CLASSIC VOLKSWAGENS

Colin Burnham

First published in 1988 by Osprey Publishing
Limited
59 Grosvenor Street, London W1X 9DA
First reprint summer 1989
Second reprint spring 1991
Third reprint summer 1992

British Library Cataloguing in Publication Data

Burnham, Colin
    Classic Volkswagens
    1. Volkswagen cars
    I. Title
    629.2′504
ISBN 0-85045-812-9

Editor Tony Thacker
Design David Tarbutt

Filmset by Tameside Filmsetting Limited,
Ashton-under-Lyne, Lancashire
Printed in Hong Kong

Front cover illustration
*Azusa's Taylor Hughes is one of the few
VW owners in California who can say
they drive on the 'wrong' side! His
immaculate 1954 right-hand-drive Beetle
was imported from England in 1986 and
treated to a flawless paintjob, new tweed
upholstery and a set of 'wide-whites'. The
car may not be completely original, but, in
the U.S.A. Taylor's driving position most
certainly is.*

Back cover illustration
*Cool convert! Burton Burton's Beryl Green
1960 model, fully restored by its previous
owner, Scott Hendrickson, and pictured at
the Royal Laundry in Pasadena. The avid
VW collector added this one to his stable
just after he acquired a '61 Sunroof in the
same colour—how could he resist? The car
has been voted 'Best Cabriolet' on several
occasions and, apparently, it was formerly
owned by an elderly Mexican gentleman
who used it to deliver newspapers in and
around east Los Angeles. A people's car
par excellence!*

Half-title illustration
*Pasadena's romantic little railway station
provides the setting for one of Burton
Burton's Oval-window Bugs. Who said it
never rains in California?*

Title-page illustration
*Built in 1957, photographed 30 years later.
What a 'Dream Machine'!*

About the author
Colin Burnham is a London-based
photojournalist who has specialized in
the automotive field for the past ten
years. His work appears regularly in
various journals in England and Europe,
and this is his second book in the
Osprey Colour Series, following
Air-cooled Volkswagens. He drives a
VW Bus.

Acknowledgement
The author has many people to thank
for their interest in this book—not
least the owners of all the vehicles
pictured—but he wishes to say a
special 'thank you' to Burton Burton,
Willi Lottermann, Jacky Morel, Chris
Morley, Clive Househam, Pan Am
World Airways, and Colorific for
providing the photo on page 9. All
other photos taken on Kodachrome 64
using Olympus 35 mm equipment

For a catalogue of all books published by Osprey Automotive
please write to:

**The Marketing Department, Octopus Illustrated Books,
1st Floor, Michelin House, 81 Fulham Road, London SW3 6RB**

Contents

*The universally-familiar symbol, as seen
on the face of a 1962 Deluxe Microbus*

Introduction

I considered this introduction to *Classic Volkswagens* whilst stuck in a traffic jam on the outskirts of London. Two possible angles came to mind. The first was based on the fact that it was almost half a century to the day since Hitler laid the foundation stone for the new 'people's car' factory—the obvious starting point. The other possible angle, however, was more 'imaginative'. Wouldn't it add that certain credence, I thought, if I was able to wax lyrical about the idiosyncrasies of my early Split-window Beetle: how the trafficators often popped out at their own free will; how the cable brakes were a constant source of anxiety, and so on. That would be the ideal intro, I thought, hunched over the wheel of my 'practical' 1974 VW Bus . . . .

Unfortunately, I have to admit that I have only ever had one 'intimate' relationship with a *classic* VW, and the vehicle in question wasn't even old enough to be an Oval-window, let alone a Split. It was a 1963 Sunroof Beetle, my first-ever Volkswagen 13 years ago. It was black, registration number *4011 KX*, and at one stage, I remember, we fitted three supposedly good engines in as many months. The odd snapshots I possess today make me wonder why I ever sold it, and why it is that every young Beetle driver loves to see how many people he or she can cram inside before the rear tyres start to rub on the wings. None of the 'late-models' that succeeded *KX* had quite the same character.

Hopefully, the contents of this book will evoke equally vivid memories for the ex-classic drivers like myself, or,

moreover, inspire you to prolong the life of your ageing air-cooled Volkswagen, however old it may be. Most of the pre-1968s pictured—in America, Germany and England—are either show-winning restorations or beautiful original examples; the *crème de la crème* from those countries. However, for all their merits, each simply serves to illustrate a passion common to thousands of VW enthusiasts around the world; a spirit that refuses to be swept along by modern-day technology. A fascination for the *people's* car.

What a cross-section of people I met while taking these pictures. From the ex-Hollywood film mogul to the unemployed ex-hippie, it soon became apparent that the ubiquitous German car really did cross all social barriers—certainly in California. And each of the owners had his own story to tell. One of the most fascinating was that of Burton Burton (not a printer's error, but the given name of a compulsive collector of classic VWs); a classic American success story. Burton had started out making ceiling fans at home in his spare time and within ten years had become president of a multi-million-dollar company whose products are now *de rigueur* in restaurants and homes right across the USA. Similarly, in less than two years, he had accumulated the finest private collection of vintage Volkswagens in the world, though not for any commercial reason—they were simply 'toys'.

I shall never forget driving some of these toys around Pasadena. Imagine being handed the keys to a warehouse full of *concours* Cabriolets, Ovals and Buses, with the only proviso being to 'take good care of 'em'. It was fun to say the least, though not without trauma. With only limited time to shoot Burton's 20-odd vehicles, my

enthusiasm was immediately dampened by the fact that there was only one good 6-volt battery amongst them, and no booster. Then, just when I became 'the fastest battery-swapper in the West', it rained. And never stopped. Still, I was lucky enough to drive a few of those old convertibles along the freeway, and for the first time I fully understood why the VW became America's most popular small car.

What hasn't been written about the Beetle and its air-cooled derivatives could be put on the back of a postage stamp, and you would still have lots of white space to play with. So if you are one of those VW *aficionados*, please don't expect to find any startling new information within these pages. My only hope is that the book serves as an enjoyable excursion into the colourful world of classic Volkswagens, one that you will wish to repeat.

Colin Burnham
London, England 1988

The people's car – the birth of a legend

More than half a century ago, work began on what was to become the world's most successful car: the *Volkswagen* or 'people's car'. Still in production in Mexico at the time of writing, the Beetle, with its unique, almost unchanging shape, has become an icon of the 20th century. Like the Coca-Cola bottle, the Xerox machine, the hammer and sickle, and even the swastika—to which it is historically related—the venerable VW is a permanent cultural artifact: a *classic* of automotive design.

Contrary to what many believe, the Volkswagen Beetle as a vehicular concept did not spring fully-formed from the mind of Ferdinand Porsche in the mid-1930s. Although the distinguished designer's contributions should not be minimized, the main characteristics of the car—swing axle,

central-tube frame, torsion-bar suspension, opposed air-cooled engine at the rear, and a streamlined body shape—had been around for decades prior to the announcement of the German people's car. The roots of this legend are as deep and as old as Hitler's decision to appoint Porsche as his *Reichskonstrukteur* in 1934. As the 'Imperial Engineer' chosen to implement the Führer's automotive vision, Porsche could not be seen as anything less than 'Germany's greatest auto designer', and it is an image which has been richly enhanced ever since, thanks to the phenomenal success of the Beetle and the VW-derived Porsche marque.

Although the Beetle's design was unconventional by American or Western European standards, it was typical of the ideas propounded by a group of engineers in the old Austro-

Hungarian Empire during the early part of the century. They included Edmund Rumpler, Hans Ledwinka, Josef Ganz and Ferdinand Porsche (born in the Czech province of Bohemia, near Prague, in 1875), and their basic premises were quite simple. The roads in that part of the world could be atrocious, so some form of independent suspension was almost essential. Winters were extremely cold, too, so air-cooling to eliminate freezing radiators was another necessity. A rear-mounted engine made sense in terms of traction on rough terrain, and besides, engines were noisy and smelly, so it was logical to put them in the back where their effect would be lessened.

Vienna-born Rumpler patented a swing-axle design as long ago as 1903, though the first production car to feature this principle was actually manufactured in the United States ten years later by the Blood Brothers of Kalamazoo, Michigan. The car was called the Cornelian but, though well publicized, its unique features left no lasting impression upon designers, manufacturers or consumers. In 1912, Porsche himself (the name derives from 'Borislav', a hero or god in Czech mythology) designed an air-cooled, opposed four-cylinder aircraft engine for Austro-Daimler, but even this was not entirely original—De Dion-Bouton had patented a similar design as far back as 1895.

Rumpler, recognizing the form of a falling drop of liquid as the ideal aerodynamic shape, unveiled his revolutionary *Tropfen-Auto* at the Berlin Auto Show in 1921: an integrated and harmonious ensemble of new ideas that would ultimately influence the design

of Porsche's small car. Likewise Tatra's sensational Type II, introduced the following year and designed by Porsche's close friend Hans Ledwinka. Like the British Rover of 1904 and the French Simplicia of 1909, this Czechoslovakian car had no frame in the conventional sense, just a large-diameter central-tube 'backbone' with cross-members welded to it supporting the coachwork. It also featured an air-cooled engine (albeit a front-mounted two-cylinder one), a Rumpler-type swing-axle rear and a light beam axle at the front. It was lightweight, economical to buy and operate, and almost indestructible—much like the Volkswagen many years later. Even the name 'Volkswagen' wasn't unique. In 1932, Standard Fahrzeugfabrik had built the Standard Superior, designed by small-car advocate Josef Ganz, with remarkably Beetle-like looks and a rear-mounted air-cooled engine. The advertisements billed it as a *Deutschen Volkswagen.*

Similarly, years before Porsche, Hitler and his adviser Jakob Werlin met in Berlin to discuss the 'small car for the nation', the German car industry, together with the press and the government, was convinced of the country's need for an everyman's car—a practical vehicle that the average German family could afford to buy and maintain. When Hitler embarked on his mission to build such a car, he was merely echoing the voice of *das Volk.*

Ferdinand Porsche is said to have been a restless man, rarely satisfied with his own achievements or those of his colleagues. Certainly, he was an extremely inventive individual from a fairly humble background. At the age of 15, when electricity was almost an unknown commodity amongst the population in his part of the world, he amazed those around him by designing

and building his own electric lighting system from scratch. This fascination with electricity led him to develop an electric-powered vehicle, the Lohner-Porsche *Elektrochaise*, in 1900. He subsequently designed a 'mixed-drive' car with a petrol engine generating power for electric motors mounted in each front wheel hub. This system, which he later incorporated in a World War 1 howitzer tractor-train, helped him to achieve honorary doctorate status at the Vienna Technical University in 1917; henceforth, he was known as Dr Porsche. His 'Professor' title came as a result of being awarded the National Culture Prize, the highest civilian accolade in Germany, in 1940.

From 1906 to 1923, Porsche was employed as technical director and later managing director of Austro-Daimler. During this period, his achievements included the development of several high-performance sportscars, various aero-engines, and other projects connected with the military. But it was after World War 1 that Porsche began to give serious consideration to the design possibilities of a low-priced, high-quality small car, ultimately for the benefit of the ordinary working man who at that time considered himself lucky if he could afford a new bicycle. Like Hitler, Porsche was a great admirer of Henry Ford, the pioneer of mass-production in the United States, whose Model T was achieving the success that the Beetle would later match and eventually surpass. Citroën of France had introduced their economical 2CV, while in England Herbert Austin had been thinking along similar lines with his 750 cc Austin 7. Austro-Daimler, however, were sticking exclusively to the luxury end of the market, and Porsche left the company somewhat acrimoniously.

His subsequent position with

Daimler Motoren in Stuttgart won fame for a series of record-setting racing cars and much prestige for the supercharged Mercedes models. However, the 1926 merger with Benz increased tensions for Dr Porsche, whose intuitive leaps and reliance on instinct rather than mathematical explanation often dismayed the rather staid board of directors. Consequently, he left by 'mutual consent'. Following a short term of employment with Steyr of Austria, Porsche, at 55, eventually formed his own consultancy in Stuttgart in 1930.

In spite of the prevailing economic gloom and high level of unemployment, Porsche once again turned his thoughts to a people's car, and in September 1931 he outlined these ideas to his small, but élite, team of specialist designers. Project 12, as it was called, would represent a fresh concept in German motoring; a small car designed specifically as such, rather than a scaled-down compromise of a larger vehicle. He stated that the four-seater should have a rear-mounted engine, eliminating the need for a driveshaft and thus avoiding the torque load this imposed. The engine, probably a lightweight, aircraft-type three-cylinder, was to be located behind the rear axle, with an integrated four-speed gearbox and differential unit to the fore of the axle. Independent suspension by means of swinging halfshafts and transverse torsion bars would provide the smooth ride and handling associated with expensive cars, while the lightweight, two-door, pressed-steel bodyshell would have to be very streamlined in order to provide good fuel consumption. Further weight reduction would be achieved through the use of a central-backbone chassis. Most importantly, production costs would have to be kept to an absolute

minimum, so that the average family could afford to buy the car—the one thing no manufacturer had yet been able to achieve. Little did Porsche suspect that this speculative project would, through a series of events largely related to Hitler's quest for supreme power, become the world's most successful production vehicle.

German motorcycle manufacturer Zündapp, seeking an alternative saleable product, provided the necessary funds to develop the first three prototypes in 1932. Although a five-cylinder water-cooled radial engine was favoured by the sponsors, many of Porsche's original specifications were included—notably, the familiar beetle-backed aerodynamic styling, swing-axle/leaf-spring rear suspension, and a fourth gear that allowed the car to cruise at a relatively high speed without over-stressing the engine. Zündapp, however, dropped the project soon after initial testing began. This setback might well have prompted Porsche to take up the offer of becoming Russia's 'State Designer', had not another German motorcycle manufacturer approached him sooner.

NSU had asked Porsche to design a small, economical *Volksauto* during the early stages of the Zündapp project, so naturally, when the latter fell through, he seized the opportunity to develop his ideas further. The subsequent NSU prototypes were the real forerunners of the Beetle, featuring most of the well-known mechanical characteristics, including a noisy 20 hp air-cooled ohv flat-four engine and the 1931-patented trailing-link torsion-bar front suspension (the latter was actually the work of Porsche's chief designer and unsung hero of the VW story, Karl Rabe). Nevertheless, this car (Project 32) also failed to reach series-production—even though by this time Porsche had met the man who, in effect, would be the ultimate benefactor for his small-car project: the new German Chancellor, Adolf Hitler.

Although he never drove, Hitler had always been car-crazy. During the earliest days of the Nazi movement, he had emptied the meagre party treasury to buy a luxury Mercedes in which to tour the country and seek political support. The salesman who sold him that Porsche-designed car was Jakob Werlin, a close friend who later became his chief adviser on motoring matters and as such played an important role in the evolution of the Volkswagen. He was also the man who drove to Landsberg prison in 1923 to pick up Hitler following a nine-month sentence for riotous behaviour. During his internment, Hitler's favourite reading matter was a biography of Henry Ford, and it is that book which is said to have inspired his ideas for a car with which to bring about the mass-motorization of the Third Reich.

The new Chancellor and the German automotive industry were brought together 11 days after his election victory on 11 February 1933, at the opening of the annual Berlin Auto Show. Against a backdrop of swastika banners and giant photos of marching storm-troopers, Hitler delivered his first significant speech to the nation. He said: 'A nation is no longer judged by the length of its railway network, but by the length of its highways.' He stressed the importance of a new first-class road network, the inexpensive mass-produced automobile, and international motor competition as a showcase for the technological competence of the nation and its people. Moreover, in his opening speech at the 1934 show, he stated that it was the intention of his

government to support the production of a *Deutschen Volkswagen*.

Porsche's first meeting with Hitler took place in March 1933, though it had no bearing on the people's car project. It was an attempt by the designer to gain financial assistance for his now-legendary Auto Union racing car. Porsche's keen interest in motor sport went right back to that first *Elektrochaise* in which he won a race at 9 mph, but this 16-cylinder mid-engined car would, he claimed, give the type of performance required to put Germany back amongst the world's leading competitors. Although Hitler did not really favour Auto Union (an anonymous amalgamation of four companies) as Germany's representative, he was sufficiently impressed by the eloquent Dr Porsche to release the coveted subsidy.

Sometime during May 1934, Jakob Werlin phoned Porsche, asking that he present himself at Berlin's Kaiserhof Hotel the following day. It was a matter of great importance, about which he could say no more over the phone. Porsche made the long journey across Germany and was greeted by Werlin, who explained that they were about to have a private audience with the Führer for the purpose of discussing a small-car programme. The three men, all from the same corner of the German-speaking world, got along well, and Hitler told Porsche what *he* wanted in the way of a '*Volkswagen*'.

He stipulated a vehicle able to accommodate two adults and three children at a cruising speed of 60 mph over his new autobahns, returning at least 33 mpg. As the majority of owners would have limited finance, the cost of general maintenance would have to be low. Likewise, since their hard day's toil began at the crack of dawn, often in sub-zero temperatures,

the engine would have to be air-cooled and extremely reliable. Thus far the designer was in agreement, but the crunch came when Hitler named the proposed selling price. This was to be below 1000 Reichsmarks—some 30 per cent cheaper than any small car available at the time, and not much more than the price of a motorcycle. It was an all-but-impossible task, as far as Porsche was concerned.

After a considerable amount of ministerial activity, Hitler came up with a scheme to keep the price down to his pre-determined, and largely 'political', figure. He ordered the scheme to be put in the hands of the RDA (the society of German auto manufacturers), whose members would undertake (willingly or otherwise) to produce the components in their factories. Dr Porsche subsequently received a communication from the Ministry of Transport containing a list of the official bodies who would be involved in the operation, with a rather significant footnote stating that the car must also be capable of carrying three soldiers and one machine-gun plus ammunition. It seems almost certain that Porsche had to agree to the car's possible military application before being offered the contract to produce the civilian version, his lifelong ambition.

The people's car project was labelled Type 60, and with only ten months to produce three prototypes, Porsche had little alternative but to use the NSU design as a basis for further development. The Stuttgart office became a hive of activity as the team grappled with the problems presented by the cost limitations. They experimented with a variety of engines, including an 850 cc vertical-twin-cylinder two-stroke and a two-cylinder Boxermotor of similar capacity. In the

The 1131 cc engine of a 1948 Beetle. This engine size was introduced into the Kübel/Schwimmwagen in 1942 and powered all Volkswagen vehicles until 1954, when the capacity was enlarged to 1192 cc and the compression raised from 5.8:1 to 6.6:1 to produce 36 bhp (SAE). The design of VW's air-cooled flat-four dates back to late 1934, when Austrian Franz Reimspiess presented the blueprints to Dr Porsche and was later awarded 100 Reichsmarks for his efforts

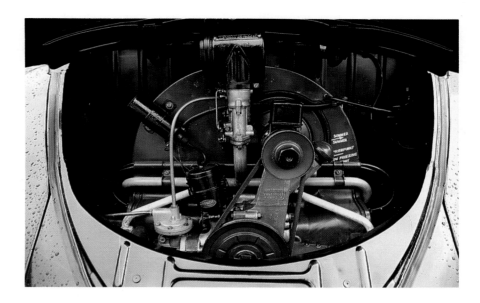

end, Porsche settled for an improved version of the flat-four NSU engine, designed by Franz Reimspiess, which actually worked out cheaper than any of the two-cylinder units. From the backbone frame of earlier prototypes came the first Beetle-like platform frame, with a pressed-steel central tube and plywood 'pan' sections between the outriggers. It was forked at the rear to form an engine cradle, with splined rear torsion bars housed in a single transverse member. At the front, the now-familiar torsion-bar suspension unit was attached to the head of the frame, carrying a worm-and-nut steering box. All in all, the first prototype chassis, though unrefined, was identical in concept to that which would later see service in all corners of the world.

By late 1935 the first complete prototype Volkswagens, V1 and V2 (convertible), were to be seen trundling up and down the new autobahns and over the Alps. Like the chassis bolted beneath them, the bodywork of these vehicles (attributed to designer Erwin Komenda) looked distinctly 'Beetle'. VW3 (three cars) followed in early 1936, and whereas cars 1 and 2 had steel bodies constructed over the traditional wooden framework, car 3 featured the first all-steel body. They were all powered by the Reimspiess

984 cc engine which developed 22 bhp at just over 3000 rpm, with a top speed of 64 mph. The now-fully-evolved platform frame was also an all-steel construction with an integrated backbone and floorpan. In October 1936, the cars were finally delivered to the RDA for road-testing and general assessment over a pre-determined distance of some 30,000 miles. Every tiny fault and occurrence was meticulously recorded and later analysed in detail. One major problem which plagued two of the cars was broken crankshafts, which were cast rather than forged. The problem was solved by fitting the latter type as used in car 3, a practice adhered to by VW ever since. Exhaust-valve failures due to over-heating was another area of concern, likewise the car's almost non-existent interior heating system. But other than that, no fundamental weaknesses or defects were discovered.

As the development programme progressed, the German auto industry, not surprisingly, became increasingly

opposed to the idea of subsidizing Hitler's brainchild. A further batch of 30 prototypes (VW30) were under construction at the Daimler-Benz factory, but the cost incurred by that stage was already well in excess of the original estimate. The RDA argued that Porsche's design could never be produced at such a ridiculously low selling price. What is more, they obviously resented the fact that they were helping to create a formidable competitor to their members' own vehicles.

Hitler, though, was adamant: the people's car must be produced as the great Dr Porsche designed it—and his eventual solution to the finance problem typified his totalitarian regime. The RDA would hand over the entire Volkswagen project to the Nazi German Labour Front (*DAF*) as 'a gesture of goodwill'. The Labour Front would then pay for the building of a factory with some of the vast contributions it collected from the millions of German workers. It would then produce the cars and sell them directly to the people, instead of the government having to subsidize the industry. The price of the car would thus be kept to the 990-mark figure by not having to pay for further development costs, factory construction costs or sales commission to dealers— and, of course, there would be no manufacturer's profit, either.

In early 1937, Hitler announced the new company in charge of Volkswagen production—*Gesellschaft zur Vorbereitung des Deutschen Volkswagen GmbH*— and it was soon known by its acronym, *Gezuvor*. Porsche was named

A trio of Split-windows at Willi Lottermann's VW-Veteranen-Treffen, staged every four years in Bad Camberg near Frankfurt. An event not to be missed!

to head the company, while Dr Bodo Lafferentz (who controlled the *Kraft durch Freude*, or 'Strength through Joy', movement of the *DAF*) and Jakob Werlin were on the board of directors. Robert Ley, head of the *Deutsche Arbeitsfront* and one of Hitler's earliest followers, was given overall responsibility. But before any form of production could begin, it was necessary to continue the car's development.

The VW30 series was subjected to more than one million miles of rigorous road tests in 1937. The project was based at an SS barracks near Stuttgart where a squad of 200 Nazi storm-troopers drove the cars in three shifts around the clock. An upright oil cooler went part-way to solving the inherent temperature problem, but the car continued to incorporate beehive-type louvering in precedence over a rear window. Various technical improvements were made as a result of this endurance test, though the general consensus was that Porsche's concept was wholly 'right'.

While all this activity was taking place in Germany, Dr Porsche and his fellow *Gezuvor* representatives visited the United States. Porsche toured the giant automobile manufacturers to examine mass-production methods and glean information on the necessary machinery, while Werlin and Lafferentz attempted to lure many of the German-born production specialists back to their homeland. Most of these skilled engineers had emigrated to the US during the post-war depression, and they were offered all kinds of incentives to return and help set up the new factory. Indeed, many did, though the majority made a hasty return when America entered World War 2 in 1941.

The plans for the Volkswagen factory were completed in January

1938, and it was to be the most ambitious undertaking of its kind anywhere in the world. A main assembly building was to stretch for almost a mile and it was planned to employ two shifts of 10,000 and 7000 men, supposedly producing upwards of half a million cars per annum. This would require an entirely new factory city to house the workers and their families in an area of about 20 square miles of flat terrain. The ideal situation for this prestigious industrial showpiece was found on the *Mittellandkanal* in Lower Saxony, between Berlin and Hanover, and construction work began in September 1938. As it worked out, and thanks to a sizeable Italian workforce provided by Hitler's fellow dictator, Mussolini, the main building took just 18 months to complete.

Meanwhile, in late 1937, Reutter, the Stuttgart coachbuilders, received an order for another 30 pre-production bodies, coded VW38. These prototypes marked the final stage of evolution for the Beetle, with specifications that would remain almost entirely unaltered until well after the war. A much-improved air-cooling system reduced the reliance on external currents, thus the body finally received its characteristic 'split' rear window. Other notable changes included the adoption of front-hinged doors with vertical (as opposed to 'canted') pillars, much larger rear side windows, and, for the first time, bumpers front and back. Hitler could finally display his long-awaited people's car to a curious German public.

The VW38s (44 were eventually built, followed by another 50 'show' cars coded VW39) were much less spartan and generally more attractive than the early prototypes, and they were later shipped around the country to entice the German public at various festivals and fairs. Saloon, Sunroof and Cabriolet models were on hand on 26 May 1938, when, amidst Nazi brass hats and brown-shirted Hitler youth, the Führer laid the cornerstone of the new factory. It was a ceremonious occasion given all the theatrical pomp that the Nazis had become so skilful at, with an estimated 70,000 people brought to the site in special buses and trains from all over the country. This included 150 reporters who would spread the story through newspapers, all controlled by the Nazi propaganda department. Hitler delivered a relatively dull and convoluted speech by his usual standards, but he ended with a surprise that awakened his listeners, including the apolitical Dr Porsche: 'The car that will be built here has been created for the people. It will serve them in their daily tasks as a means of transport and will bring them joy in their leisure. The car, therefore, shall bear the name of the 'Strength through Joy' movement which made all this possible. It shall be known as the *KdF-Wagen*.'

Hitler, of course, had always been aware of the political capital to be made out of such emotive issues as private-car ownership. In his vociferous speech at the 1934 Berlin Auto Show, pounding on the lectern in his usual manic style, he decried the fact that Germany had only one car for each 50 inhabitants, compared to one for every five in the United States. A *Wagen* was simply an unattainable dream for the bulk of the electorate—but their leader was seen to be making it a future reality. The price of the state-subsidized KdF car was to be fixed at RM990 (plus RM60 for the Sunroof version), which, at 500 marks less than the cheapest car available at the time (General Motors' Opel P4), made it unbelievably *cheap*. However, that figure still amounted to almost half a

year's wages for the average German worker, so it was unlikely there would have been many cash customers queuing up even if the car had been immediately available (production was due to commence in September 1939—the month in which World War 2 was declared). Robert Ley, therefore, devised a rather ingenious savings scheme that would enable every German worker to own a KdF 'limousine'; much like a hire-purchase agreement, but in reverse.

The scheme, which came into effect on 1 January 1939, required the would-be buyers to commit themselves to the purchase of at least five Reichsmarks' worth of savings stamps each week, to be affixed in a savings book which had to be exchanged for a new one when full. The saver was also entitled to purchase more stamps at any one time, even up to the full value of the car. For young people or those on very low incomes, there was a reduced savings plan which could be increased when incomes rose. Mandatory insurance cover for two years cost a further RM200, and the contract could not be cancelled without forfeiting *all* that had been paid in. A single default on the payments had the same consequence. Furthermore, there was no interest payable on the money invested which, at the minimum weekly payments, would be in the hands of the KdF for more than four years. Some 337,000 faithfuls put their names to this scheme, which led to the accumulation of more than 280 million Reichsmarks through the war years. But paradoxically, it was *not* a giant con-trick to raise funds for military purposes, since every last *Pfennig* was deposited by the KdF in the Bank of German Labour in Berlin— which was seized by the Russians at the end of the war. And though the savers never did receive their cars, they

were in fact offered some recompense by VW in 1961 (albeit after 12 years of legal proceedings) in the form of DM100 cash or DM600 off the price of a new Volkswagen. Almost half of them chose the rebate.

By late 1938, though, the war clouds were once again gathering over Europe. Two months before the cornerstone ceremony, Hitler had sent his troops into his native Austria to achieve the *Anschluss*, the union of Austria with Germany in the Third Reich. Britain and France, the isolated democracies in a Europe riddled with dictatorships, had had to accept his sarcastic declaration: 'We move through the world as a peace-loving angel, but one armed in iron and steel.' On 3 October, the Führer crossed the former border into Sudetenland in his four-wheel-drive Mercedes, and on 15 March 1939 he occupied the rest of Czechoslovakia. In a year, with scarcely a shot fired, he had added some ten million people to Germany—though the most devastating war in history was but a few months away. The 'proprietary pride' that the *New York Times* called Hitler's feeling about the people's car was completely eclipsed by his dream of the new, greater Germany. Furthermore, the hopes of millions of ordinary working people began to fade as the KdF-Wagen's military application began to take precedence . . . .

The early years (1939-1952)

Although Ferdinand Porsche was never politically inclined, his flair for mechanical design played an important role in Hitler's New Order. By the outbreak of World War 2, Porsche and his team of specialists found themselves fully occupied with a never-ending list of military requirements. These included numerous tank designs and aero-engines, and a variety of four-wheeled vehicles not only designed to transport Hitler's armies across conquered territories, but also to ensure their full mobility in the most extreme conditions. Needless to say, these military *Wagens* were based on the already fully-developed people's car chassis, and they proved beyond doubt that the air-cooled Volkswagen was both rugged and dependable—though it would be several years before the rest of the world would come to appreciate the rear-engined oddity . . . .

The first Volkswagen-based cross-country vehicle was built a good two years before Britain and France declared war against Germany. It was a basic 'tub' on a prototype VW30 chassis, and was followed by the first rounded, then angular, Type 62—the forerunner of the ubiquitous wartime 'Kübelwagen', or Type 82. Some 50,000 of these lightweight open 'bucket cars' were produced at the KdF car plant through the war years, and the vehicle became as dear to the hearts of German troops as the Jeep was to Americans— particularly General Rommel's fabled *Afrika Korps.* With reduction gears at the rear hubs and modified stub axles, the corrugated Kübel featured 11 in. of ground clearance and, with the aid of a limited-slip differential, would scramble through the mud and sand much like its four-wheel-drive American

counterpart. What is more, being 650 lb lighter, it was easily manoeuvrable when it eventually ran aground. The four-door four-seater, initially with the VW38 985 cc engine but later to incorporate 1131 cc, quickly spawned a number of variants, including a *Schneeraupe* (snow caterpillar) featuring half-tracks on bogey wheels at the back.

The newly-built Volkswagen car plant must have appeared right from the outset as the perfect armaments factory, but there is no evidence to suggest that this was Hitler's intention. According to Albert Speer, the wartime armaments minister and former architect, Hitler was by no means prepared for a full-scale war and there was utter chaos at the plant when the news was declared. Volkmar Köhler, the factory's historian, reiterates this view and claims that the biggest production job it received during the war was the manufacturing of tens of thousands of sheet-metal stoves to warm troops on the Russian Front. What can be ascertained is that the control of the KdF factory was transferred from the Labour Front to the Reich Air Ministry, under Hermann Göring, and used as an aircraft facility. By 1943, the plant was manned by an estimated 12,500 undernourished prisoners of war, mainly repairing damaged wings, tail assemblies, and so on, for the all-powerful *Luftwaffe*. The Kübelwagen assembly-line occupied a very small portion of the factory floor, since all the components apart from the engine and transmission were manufactured by outside suppliers. The factory managed to escape heavy bombardment right up until the end of the war.

In 1942, the Kübel was joined by the amphibious, all-wheel-drive 'Schwimmwagen', or Type 166, a development of an earlier Porsche design known as the Type 128. The Schwimmer had a 16 in. shorter wheelbase than the Kübel or KdF-Wagen (Beetle), not to mention several refinements to the drivetrain and seals, and about 15,000 were produced. It moved through the water by means of a special reduction gear-driven propeller in the stern of its boat-like bodyshell. The hinged three-bladed prop could be flipped down to engage a drive clutch from the crankshaft whenever the vehicle was ready to enter the water. Carburettor air-intake and exhaust outlets were positioned high and dry on the 'deck', and under ideal conditions it could slosh through the water at 15 mph. The amphibian was officially designed for reconnaissance duties, but when it proved ideal for planing over Russian snow, Professor Porsche was obliged to accept honorary SS membership. Also, in 1942, the scarcity of light alloys led Porsche to design an engine cooling fan cut from sheet metal, to replace the original cast model. Necessity being the mother of invention, it was discovered that these new blades produced a lot more air-flow and, as an added bonus, they were also much quieter.

As well as the variety of offshoots to come from the Kübel and Schwimmwagen, the KdF-Wagen continued to exist in both military and civilian form, although the latter, totalling a mere 630 units, was little more than a token gesture to the thousands who continued to buy their savings stamps. Type 82E was designated to a KdF body affixed to a Kübel chassis, and this is sometimes referred to as a 'command car'. However, the real *Kommandeurwagen*

was the Type 87: a KdF body bolted on the early full-length-wheelbase (94.6 in.), four-wheel-drive Type 128 chassis. There were other variations, too, with equally esoteric tags. Altogether, 667 of these specialized Beetles were built between 1942 and 1944. Other notable wartime developments at Porsche's Stuttgart offices included attempts at supercharging, turbocharging and fuel-injecting the 30 hp (SAE) flat-four, and for some reason they even tried a diesel variant. Automatic-transmission possibilities were also explored, as was a fully-synchronized five-speed manual gearbox. Perhaps the most unlikely

state-financed project of all, though, was a light off-road carry-all with six wheels and two VW engines! But like so many of Porsche's highly inventive ideas, it never went further than the prototype stage.

By the end of the war, the factory was reportedly being used for the construction of airframes and, moreover, the manufacture of the unmanned V-1 'buzz bomb'. This prompted the first of several major bombing raids by the US Air Force in April 1944. Orders were subsequently received at the factory to protect the machinery in any way possible, and most of it was transferred to the

Looking for all the world like the start of the classic Le Mans 24 Hours race, the combined horsepower of these vintage VWs probably wouldn't equal a modern-day Porsche racer, but they would certainly have the reliability to go the full distance

factory basement or to dispersal sites in the surrounding countryside, where it remained in use. A few months later, more than 2000 V-1s hit London, killing 4000 people and injuring many thousands more. The Allies were then determined more than ever to stop them at source. Two massive daylight raids were made by US bombers in June, followed by another in August

which left the factory in ruins, though most of the machinery survived. Unlike Hitler, who committed suicide on 30 April 1945.

Germany's near-total collapse was all too evident at *KdF-Stadt* at the close of war. Two-thirds of the massive showpiece had been devastated and the remaining workforce were completely demoralized. Fortunately, though, under the Allied plan to divide the country into four separate Occupation Zones, the factory was put in the hands of the British Army, whose gallant efforts and all-round ingenuity would pave the way for Volkswagen's future success. One of their first moves, however, was to appoint an embryo town council

Shortly after the initial production run of KdF civilian cars in 1938, Hitler's totalitarian regime meant that Dr Porsche was forced to abandon the development of his people's car in favour of a lightweight vehicle for military purposes. It was based, needless to say, on the rigorously-tested Volkswagen chassis and became known as the Kübelwagen or 'bucket car'. More than 50,000 were produced between 1940 and early 1945. Its special features included a limited-slip differential for better traction,

reduction gears and modified stub axles for greater ground clearance, and a unique hydraulic steering damper which allowed the steering wheel to rise and fall over rough terrain. With its reliable air-cooled engine, the Kübel proved to be one of Hitler's greatest assets during World War 2—as capable in the severe heat of the North African desert as in the sub-zero temperatures of the Russian Front. Witness Hans Schuckenböhmer's example, pictured in a contemporary West German setting

Above

In 1942, Porsche came up with the answer to a request from the Wehrmacht (German Army) for an amphibious jeep: the Type 166 Schwimmwagen. Schwimmers have four-wheel drive, and a propeller which can be engaged once afloat

Left

Wait for it ... an exact replica of one of the earliest pre-war prototype Type 62s, circa 1938. This odd-looking creature went through a metamorphosis and eventually became the Kübelwagen. And no, it's not available in kit form ...

which at their first meeting officially named the town Wolfsburg.

Civilian road transport in war-torn Germany was at a virtual standstill, so the initial effort called for repairs to trucks and buses. But it was not long before the British realized the potential for producing Volkswagens as light transport for the occupying forces. Major Ivan Hirst of the REME (Royal Electrical and Mechanical Engineers) was brought in by the Military Government in mid-1945 to assess the situation and it became clear that if the necessary materials and components could be obtained, production of the

Beetle—virtually an unknown commodity to the British at this time—could be started. Once a 'demonstrator' had been commandeered and sent to Army HQ for general assessment, the decision was made: an order for 5000 saloons was placed with the factory. Hitler's dream was finally on the road to reality.

Early Volkswagen production was an *ad hoc* affair while the plant was being rebuilt, re-equipped and generally reorganized, and outside suppliers were being re-activated. Amidst tons of rubble and twisted metal, the cars were made up with whatever was available

from old stocks. The first 2500 built in 1945 all had Kübelwagen chassis parts which gave them a *Kommandeur*-type stance, and their roofs consisted of two panels welded together until sufficiently large sheets of steel could be obtained. The supply of carburettors from Solex in Berlin soon ran out, and until Solex of Paris developed a replacement, in late 1947, the cars featured a 'pirate' carb with several of its smaller parts produced by a nearby camera firm. Fish glue was used in the trim; this, it was later discovered, resulted in a somewhat distasteful odour. Likewise the smell of burning oil, the result of

Left
The ubiquitous air-cooled, horizontally-opposed flat-four, the most celebrated car engine of this century

Below
What better car for a fitness freak than a '49 Volkswagen? This shining example could be one of the first two sedans exported to the US in late 1949, but more likely it was shipped over sometime later by the kind of freak you're likely to meet at VW Classic, the premier VW event in California

an inferior solder used in the manufacture of the oil cooler. More seriously, a design fault in the steering box resulted in a number of fatal accidents. But gradually the bugs were ironed out, and by the end of March 1946 the initial target of 1000 cars per month had been reached—all 'normal' Type 11 (later changed to Type 1) Beetles. Almost 8000 cars had been built by the end of that year, and but for a few 'oddballs' required by essential services, all were absorbed by the Allied requirement.

Labour at Wolfsburg in the early days consisted largely of former German prisoners of war who, on their release, were offered the work through the manpower division of the CCG (Control Commission for Germany). The conditions, however, were primitive—both inside and outside the factory—and the rapid turnover of workers was a major problem. Similarly, the German management (under British control) changed frequently as personnel came to be dismissed under the de-Nazification process (forbidding any ex-Nazi to have supervision over fellow Germans).

But the biggest cloud which hung over the factory during those early years was the threat of dismantling for reparations. War plants were automatically dismantled, while tooling from other installations listed as 'surplus to post-war German industry' was also made available to the Allies as reparation (i.e. any of the Allies could bid for it). Since Wolfsburg had originally and quite genuinely been built for civilian production, it was not classified as a 'war plant' (a 'powerful political weapon', perhaps), but it *was* listed under the second heading. Fortunately, the British managed to place a four-year reserve on the factory in 1945 (based on the fact that the Allied authorities needed transportation while in occupation), and by the time this period had elapsed, the 'level of industry' plan had been scrapped— yet another stroke of luck for the people's car.

Being ex-Nazi property, the Wolfsburg Motor Works (as it was known under the British) was placed in the hands of 'Property Control' at CCG headquarters, whose prime function was to look after the assets of individuals who had fled from Germany. This meant, in effect, that Volkswagen as a company was controlled by a British board of directors until it was officially handed back to the Federal Republic in September 1949. Stories about the VW concern being offered to the British motor industry—Sir William Rootes, in particular—are pure myth, since it was not available anyway. Rootes did visit the factory shortly after the war, but he merely told Hirst: 'If you think you're going to get that car back into production, then you're a fool!' or words to that effect. Henry Ford was another automotive celebrity who, the Germans have since claimed, declined the offer of the Volkswagen Beetle. In

actual fact, Henry Ford II visited Germany in March 1948 and dismissed any vague possibility of a future takeover as soon as he looked at a map. Wolfsburg was much too close to the East German border.

By 1947, the political climate was changing and the Allies realized that they needed a stronger German economy. The bill for essential imports had been high and the German Reichsmark was worthless as an international currency; consequently, each Occupation Zone had been a heavy financial burden on the respective countries' taxpayers. German companies were thus encouraged to export their products to help pay their way. As the Allied requirements had been satisfied, Beetles began to appear in German showrooms priced at around 5000 Reichsmarks, a large number being bought by American and British servicemen, and the first foreign concessionaire was established in Holland. Further foreign interest came as a result of the car's first bonafide launch at the 1947 Hanover Fair. It soon became apparent to the British board that VW could have a viable future as a major car manufacturer, though the threat of reparations was still in the air.

Below & overleaf

Heinz-Willi Lottermann, Volkswagen dealer, collector and enthusiast, staged his first vintage VW meeting in his home-town of Bad Camberg, near Frankfurt, in 1979. It was so successful that he decided to repeat the event—not annually, but every four years. The next three-day meeting in 1983 attracted even more classic Volkswagens, around 140 in all, and well over 1000 enthusiasts from all corners of Europe. So it was, in June 1987, that more than 200 of the earliest and rarest VWs in the world converged upon this old German spa town for the third VW-Veteranen-Treffen. Only pre-1958 Volkswagens were invited and most were Ovals or Splits, though there were enough special bodies and military vehicles in attendance to excite even the most seasoned show-goer. Not to mention all the rare parts, toys and literature on offer in the swap-meet area of the main staging ground, half a mile from Autohaus Lottermann. Entry was free for spectators and the organization throughout the weekend was a credit to Heinz-Willi and his finely-tuned team of helpers. On Sunday, all the cars drove out into the picturesque Taunus countryside and the event ended with a huge banquet in the main Marktplatz in the centre of town. The next one is in 1991—don't miss it!

Considerable progress had been made in a relatively short space of time, both in terms of production and management, and with the arrival of ex-Opel General Manager Heinz Nordhoff, things really started to move. Major Hirst was actually looking for a deputy manager when he met with Nordhoff in 1947, but he was so impressed by his depth of knowledge of the car industry, not to mention his technical ability, he offered him the post of *Generaldirektor*. And it was under Nordhoff's direction that Volkswagenwerk GmbH became Europe's number-one car manufacturer.

The modest Major Hirst maintains to this day that the Beetle's post-war resurrection was the result of a team effort, with British and Germans pulling together. Certainly, the car was reborn through necessity. The Kübel was ruled out—the body supplier, Ambi Budd of Berlin, had been completely destroyed—and the press tools for the Beetle were largely intact. Couple that with the fact that a senior officer, Colonel McEvoy, already favoured the design (having seen it at the Berlin Auto Show before the war), and it becomes clear that the car does not owe its existence to chance—not completely, anyway. By the time Nordhoff took control in January 1948, most of the VW hallmarks such as good after-sales service and parts availability were already part of the company policy—as was the famous V-over-W emblem. It was now up to the Germans to build on well-laid foundations . . . .

When Nordhoff first took over the running of Wolfsburg (he remained the autocrat for 20 years), he regarded the Volkswagen with the utmost scepticism. It was a car that had been tarred with the brush of political

trickery, and as a marketable product it left much to be desired. But he could see its potential, and the job presented him with an irresistible challenge. In almost no time, the Volkswagen became not only part of, but central to, German recovery. It symbolized the economic miracle that transformed the country from demoralization and defeat into a nation that could, in peace if not in war, challenge and compete successfully with the nations of the world.

On 20 June 1948, Germany introduced new monetary reform laws aimed at ending the country's early post-war inflation and creating a stable economy. The old Reichsmark was withdrawn and replaced by the Deutschmark at an exchange rate of 10 : 1. While the news came as

Right
JLT 420, *an ex-CCG 1947 Beetle, was one of the first Volkswagens to find its way across the English Channel after the war. Moreover, it was the first to fall into the hands of the late John Colborne-Baber, a Surrey-based motor trader who subsequently bought up many of the early VWs brought back by ex-servicemen and later obtained the first licence to import the people's car into Britain. Part of Colborne-Baber's initial sales effort, however, was to respray and retrim those rather austere-looking post-war cars—hence JLT's two-tone paint scheme and 'Deluxe' bumpers and side trim. In many ways, this is the car that initiated VW's huge success in the UK, and some 300,000 miles later it is once again in the possession of Colborne Garages Ltd, albeit the only air-cooled relic in their plush showroom*

Left

Every VW enthusiast knows that the Beetle has proved itself time and time again in off-road competition—but no, Randy Ingersoll is not about to go boonie-bashing in this period piece! The backdrop—Palm Desert, California—just happens to be within a few hundred yards of his house where he keeps no less than a dozen air-cooled Volkswagens (not to mention a mountain of spare parts and general VW paraphernalia). Indeed, Randy is the proverbial 'VW freak', and this rare 1950 Sunroof is his most cherished possession. The old Bug—one of only 324 sold in the US that year—was actually traded in for a brand-new sedan back in 1966. But whereas most 16-year old trade-ins find new keepers quickly, 'Indio VW', not surprisingly, gave shelter to this gem until the right person came along almost 16 years later! Randy paid $5000 for the '50 (more than three times the price of a new '66) and apart from the front fenders, upholstery and many accessories, it's exactly as it was when it came from Wolfsburg almost 40 years ago. Bearing in mind that 1950 marked the beginning of an era in which American eccentricities demanded progressively bigger cars with gaudy chrome, tail-fins and powerful V8 engines, whoever bought this car brand-new must have been a true individual

something of a shock to the well-heeled sector of the community, it brought about a new stimulus to the economy as a whole; similarly, the introduction of the American Marshall Plan the same year, whereby millions of dollars were pumped into the West German treasury. These two events inspired a new air of confidence within the country and, in turn, a prosperity which directly affected Volkswagen sales. Almost 15,000 German people attained their 'dream' cars in 1948, though within three years there were more than ten times that number on the autobahns—a fact which is said to have amazed Professor Porsche, who died in 1951, aged 75.

Nordhoff concentrated on forming a closely integrated system between management and factory staff, and his 'human' approach earned great respect from the workforce. However, the ever-increasing influx of new personnel soon created a housing problem at Wolfsburg. This, like so many of the initial stumbling blocks, was overcome with typical Teutonic efficiency, and later on VW even formed a factory-financed housing construction company, operated as a Volkswagenwerk subsidiary. The town, which had previously consisted of a small handful

of buildings surrounded by a motley collection of wooden huts and muddy unpaved streets, soon expanded into a thriving community with all the amenities that Hitler had once promised. The workforce grew from 10,000 in 1949 to 20,000 by 1953.

Though there was a marked increase in output shortly after Nordhoff's arrival, considerable investment was needed to raise production to profitable levels—and exports were the key by which to obtain the necessary modern machinery from the US. 'The General' wasted no time in expanding VW's export programme, nor in improving the product. The 1948 Beetle was virtually identical to the pre-war VW38, and he called together many of its original creators to completely up-date what was, ten years later, all too basic'. Of course, they did not change the concept of the car in any way, but merely refined it, a process which continued for 30 years at Wolfsburg.

Many of the first 1131 cc engines 'died' within 30,000 miles (50,000 km), prompting Nordhoff to offer a gold watch and dash plaque to any Beetle driver who covered 100,000 km on one engine (this practice was dropped in 1958, for obvious reasons). Early improvements included

The characteristic split rear window was replaced by the one-piece oval in March 1953. This change prompted a brisk trade in cutting the centre bars out of older cars, thereby up-dating them. What sacrilege!

thermostatically-controlled vents for faster warm-up, redesigned cooling ribs and better cylinder heads, and in 1949 a higher phosphor content in the cylinders extended their life considerably. Bi-metal pistons and armoured exhaust valves were introduced along with an electron crankcase in 1951, and oil consumption was reduced in small, steady increments. Gearing and axle ratios were largely left as Porsche's Karl Fröhlich had originally designed them, likewise the chassis and suspension until telescopic dampers were fitted (front only) in 1949 and the torsion bars redesigned the following year. But the most praised change came in April 1950 when the 'Deluxe' or 'Export' model (introduced in July 1949, and always the superior model compared to the 'Standard') received much-needed hydraulic brakes. As these changes took place, the ever-increasing number of *Käfer* (Beetle) drivers were able to identify the year of each other's cars. For instance, 1948 Beetles were recognizable by the large 'VW' emblems on the hub caps, flat bumpers with banana-shaped overriders, and 'L'-type handles on both lids. A year later, the bumpers were changed to a grooved design and a cable release for the bonnet meant that the handle was fixed. Such were the VW model changes.

Above
Early 1952 Deluxe Beetle, one of the first to feature chrome trim around the windshield and a Wolfsburg crest on the hood. And one of the last to be fitted with 16 in. wheels. The twin foglights, horns, Export-specification indicators and headlight eyebrows are all owner add-ons

Above right
For a few marks more, you could have a radio (or clock) fitted in the nearside fascia panel of your brand-new 1949 Volkswagen. This Telefunken set, which features a hook-up for an external speaker (for camping and picnicking), resides in one of the '49s that were converted by Hebmüller

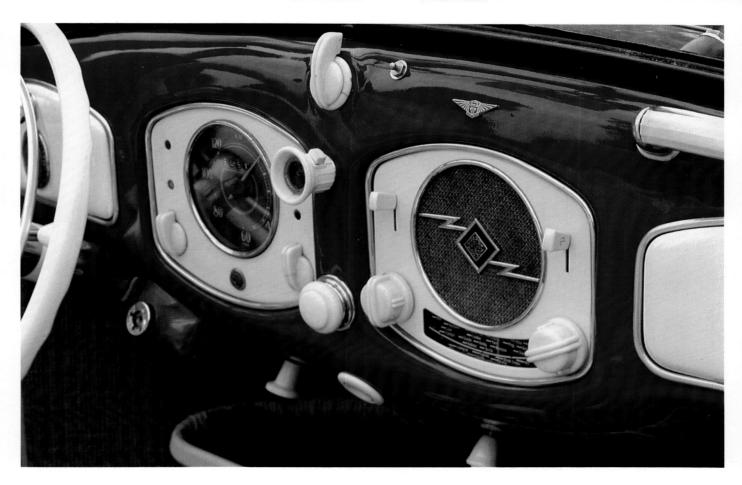

Total exports in 1948 amounted to 4464 cars—to Holland, Belgium, Switzerland and Luxembourg—and this figure was increased by some 2500 when Denmark and Sweden were added to the list in 1949. That was also the year that VW's Dutch importer, Ben Pon, attempted to raise interest in the Beetle in the world's largest car market, the USA. But to no avail. His single VW demonstrator was looked upon as nothing more than a joke on four wheels—with all-too-sinister undertones. Nordhoff himself tried to enlist American dealers, reputedly armed with nothing more than a bunch of photographs. He was also unsuccessful. The following year,

however, a leading importer of sports and luxury cars in New York agreed to sell the Volkswagen, and though Max Hoffman only managed to sell 352 'Bugs' in 1950, it marked the beginning of VW's colossal success in the US—their greatest achievement. Meanwhile, in Dublin, Ireland, Stephen O'Flaherty had the honour of seeing his company, Motor Distributors Ltd, build the first Beetle outside Germany on a new assembly-line using knocked-down cars imported from Wolfsburg (import restrictions in Britain were not lifted until 1953). South Africa followed suit a year later, in 1951, and in 1952 Volkswagen set up a sales organization in Canada. March 1953 saw knocked-

down Beetles being reassembled by *Volkswagen do Brazil* (which soon became the second-ranking producer), and two years later the same system was operating in Australia. Less than ten years after the fall of the Third Reich, the people's car was selling all around the world.

Since there were no shareholders in the VW organization at this time, all profits from export and domestic sales were ploughed back into the company, and it paid big dividends. The 1949 production figure was almost doubled in 1950 to over 90,000, some 30,000 of which went for export. By October 1952, a quarter of a million Beetles had been produced since the war. Virtually

Line 'em up! The Belgian Split in the foreground is one of the rare Standard models issued with chrome bumpers and door handles. For the most part, early Standards were as 'plain Jane' as you could get—no side trim, painted hub caps, black wiper arms and dashboard hardware—though they could be ordered with a sunroof from 1950 onwards

every German town had an authorized VW dealer, and under the rules initiated by the British and subsequently enforced by Nordhoff, each was required to carry a comprehensive stock of spares ranging from the tiniest components to a complete bodyshell. A 'fixed charge' system for servicing and repairs was

established, and a manual giving advice on correct selling techniques was made available to showroom staff—not that they really needed it in those early years, since most other German car manufacturers were still trying to recover from the effects of wartime hostilities. Nevertheless, Porsche's, and indeed Hitler's, dream of seeing the

people's car rolling off an assembly-line in vast numbers—just like Henry Ford's Model T—had finally become a reality.

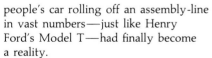

This little display would probably pay for a decent vacation in Hawaii, as would the next guy's ...

Left

Back in 1951 Tony Levy was working in Germany, and because his work involved a lot of driving he decided to buy himself an economical people's car—that is, the one he's posing with here, nearly 40 years and 850,000 miles later! It's a remarkable relationship between man and machine, made all the more noteworthy by the fact that Tony, who now lives near London, is not a typical 'enthusiast'. He bought the car for work, found it took him where he wanted to go—often more than 50,000 miles a year—and rarely let him down. He has never bothered to work on the Beetle himself and is now so used to driving it that he wouldn't dream of changing it for anything else. But amazingly, Rattletrap (as he calls it) is not the highest-mileage VW in the world. That title belongs to California's Albert Klein whose '63 Bug passed the million-mile mark in 1987

Below

Tony's car first saw the light of day in 1950, as one of a batch of 100 Spezial Produktion Beetles eventually offered to personnel of the US Occupation Forces in Germany. It had experimental rear lights, bumpers, dashboard, hydraulic brakes, quarter lights and other features not introduced as standard on Deluxe models until at least two years later. Amazingly, in covering what is roughly the equivalent of two return trips to the moon, this Wolfsburg wonder has worn out just three

Left
There are more than 36 horses in this engine, for sure. Note the supercharger and dual extractor exhaust

Below
The intricacies of screwdriver design . . .

engines and one transmission. The original 1131 cc unit managed around 280,000 miles before seizing due to a sudden loss of oil. This was followed by an 1192 cc engine, which broke up through 'sheer exhaustion' in 1971 after carrying the owner a further 238,000 miles. Volkswagen (GB) then donated another 1200 cc unit in exchange for publicity services, and that finally gave up in 1978 after another 226,000 miles. A 1300 cc engine was then fitted, two years before the original transmission eventually 'disintegrated into a handful of powdered metal. . . .' Tony's Split-window is truly a classic VW, made more so by the fact that the owner continues to use it as it was intended, as everyday transport

Restored '54 flying along the freeway

Oval windows (1953-1957)

By the end of October 1952, the number of improvements made to the Beetle were such that VW's engineers claimed there was scarcely a single part identical to the Porsche original, though the characteristic 'split' rear window was still evident. But on 10 March 1953 this was replaced by a single pane of oval-shaped glass. This profound visual change marked the beginning of Volkswagen's 'Golden Era'.

Common wisdom holds that each year's model changes occurred during the factory's annual August shut-down, in which case the introduction of the 'Oval-window' in March must seem like a minor historical aberration. In fact, the 'August' system did not come into effect until 1955, and a good third of the 200 or so changes made during the 1950s fell in other months. Those that occurred in August (signifying the next year's model) were usually the more sales-worthy features—unlike, say, an improved seal or bearing, which would be phased in immediately. Having said that, it took a real fanatic

to spot the changes made between March 1953 and August 1957. At that time, Volkswagenwerk were more interested in improving sales.

A few months after the introduction of the Oval, VW celebrated total sales of half a million, and by 1954 they had moved up to fourth place among the world's car makers, only outstripped by the American giants. Before the US went Volkswagen-crazy towards the end of the 1950s, VW's best export market was Sweden, where the Beetle actually outsold all British imports combined. Wolfsburg workers received their first annual 'success bonus' in 1954 and soaring sales were also

'D' is for Deutschland or Das Vaterland, whichever you prefer. This period accessory is a 'must' amongst early Beetle buffs, both in Germany and the USA

Left

Aftermarket accessories were available for Volkswagens as long ago as the late 1940s, offering individuality at a time when most new cars in Germany were virtually identical Beetles. One of the most popular pieces was the luggage rack—a necessity, in fact, when Herr & Frau Schmidt and family went touring

Below

Dave and Christine Evans drove their 1956 Oval through France, Belgium and Germany to be part of the small English contingent at Bad Camberg

Left

*Probably the best-known Beetle on the
Swedish show circuit, Ulf Kaijser's unique
Oval sports no less than 48 genuine 1950s
accessories! Fender skirts, sun-visor, pop-
out side windows, auxiliary lamp, wind
deflectors, headlight eyebrows ... the list
goes on. What's more, he has another 50-
odd extras at home—though he won't be
adding them to this Jungle Green '56.
The art of 'accessorizing' is knowing
when to stop*

Below left

*Ulf has owned this truly Deluxe VW for
18 years—since his 18th birthday, in
fact—and has been collecting period add-
ons since 1977. Apart from swap-meets
and 'wanted' ads in magazines, a good
source has proved to be some of the small-
town VW dealerships in Germany where,
presumably, the doo-dads were just
gathering dust. But don't assume that this
is one of those show cars that rarely sees
the light of day. No way. Every summer
the adventurous Swede embarks on a long
touring holiday in this Beetle and his
travels have taken him right across Europe.
He says he'd love to ship the car to
California and cruise along the Pacific
Coast Highway. Now that really would be
grand touring*

Right

*Nifty '50s: that's the effect you get when
you add fender skirts and 'wide-whites' to
an early Bug*

reflected in the company's annual turnover which exceeded one million Deutschmarks for the first time. Incentives to work were matched by incentives to buy, with employees being offered special discounts on the cars they helped to build—not that those in-house sales were really needed, since every other vehicle on Germany's roads was a Beetle.

January 1954 saw the first power increase since the war, when the engine displacement was increased from 1131 cc to 1192 cc and the compression raised from 5.8 : 1 to 6.6 : 1 to produce 36 hp (SAE) at 3400 rpm—a full 20 per cent increase. Speed limits were about to be abolished on the autobahns, and the *Käfer* had to do better than its previous 100 km/h (62 mph) in order to keep up. This engine managed 68 mph and ran quieter, too, thanks to a dynamically-balanced fan. Inside, a three-way courtesy light was a welcome addition, likewise a combined ignition and starter switch which replaced the starter button used previously. In 1954 also, export sales topped 100,000 for the first time, and VW's advertising literature—often lavishly illustrated in a style that would have done justice to the world's most elegant classics—depicted the Beetle in every conceivable situation. Location shots pictured the car traversing the white sands of Mexico, the Badlands of Dakota, a mountain pass in Scandinavia, or travelling somewhere in central London.

The price of a new Beetle actually dropped during the 1950s—from DM5450 in 1951 to DM4600 by 1958—as the car went 'international', causing more than a little consternation among VW's European rivals. This was partially due to Chancellor Erhardt's

Above
Of all the goodies on his car, this is Ulf's favourite: an American-made Judson supercharger. Road & Track *tested a Judson-blown Beetle in 1957 and recorded 0–60 mph in 18 seconds and a top speed of 84 mph, a big improvement over standard*

Right
A spare-wheel tool kit is one of the top items on the vintage wish list. Ulf's cared-for collection (circa 1951) would fetch close to $500 in the US

generous tax concessions on exported goods, and it led to the imposition of strict import controls in various countries to try to stem the tide of what was, by then, the world's most popular small car.

Beetle sales in Britain were minimal during the 1950s. By tradition, Britain had always been a nation of small-car producers and the loyalties of its motoring public remained firmly on the side of the domestic manufacturers following the war—certainly, it took a brave man to be seen driving a product of Hitler's Germany. However, a fair number of ex-servicemen brought back those early post-war Beetles, and many of these cars were later acquired by a Surrey motor trader, the late John Colborne-Baber, Britain's first VW

specialist. After taking *JLT 420* in part-exchange for a Buick in 1948, Colborne-Baber, convinced of the car's sales potential, placed adverts in *The Motor* and *Autocar* offering to purchase ex-CCG cars, together with the special 'parts packs' that were supplied to owners taking their cars outside Germany. He 'customized' these army-green machines—a respray and leather upholstery—to make them more attractive, and in 1951 they sold for £410, or £425 if converted to right-hand drive. Meanwhile, Colonel McEvoy, the REME officer who first saw the potential of building Volkswagens as light transport for the Allies in 1945, was granted a franchise to import spare parts into England with Colborne Garage acting as the retail

outlet. After selling around 100 of his refurbished Beetles, Colborne-Baber was granted the first franchise to sell new cars in Britain in 1952—though his import licence restricted these sales to foreign visitors only, notably US Air Force personnel stationed nearby. Although he only sold about 20 new cars that year, Colborne-Baber's unending enthusiasm for the VW led him to form the Volkswagen Owners Club of Great Britain and publish a newsletter entitled *Beetling*. The world's first all-Volkswagen magazine, incidentally, was *Gute Fahrt*, first published in Germany as early as 1950.

The nickname 'Beetle' was the obvious description for Dr Porsche's creation, and it has been said that Porsche himself originally specified a

Left
'Show 'n' Shine' fever is evident at VW events the world over. This was Stanford Hall, England, in 1987

Below
English enthusiast at the 1985 VW Action event

body shape 'streamlined as a May beetle'. Although this tale is unconfirmed, there is proof that the *New York Times* first used the description as early as 1 July 1942, and the word also appeared in Gordon Wilkins' VW article in *The Motor* of 8 May 1946. Much later, in an article in the *Chicago Heights, Illinois Star*, Roy Newquist wrote: 'Only the Volkswagen which resembles a pregnant beetle, and the Rolls-Royce, which suggests a large bank account, seem to have any individuality whatsoever.'

While Colborne-Baber played a major role in publicizing the name of the car in Britain, it was Stephen O'Flaherty who acquired the UK concessionaireship in 1953. The Irishman's London-based company, VW Motors, soon received a number of applications from would-be distributors and dealers in spite of the prevailing anti-German sentiment (there was a distinct shortage of new cars in Britain at that time), and by the end of 1954 had sold more than 4000 cars. However, some 75 per cent of these Volkswagens were vandalized in some way, which reflected the general feeling in Britain towards '*that* German car'. By 1957, the memories of wartime hostilities were beginning to fade as the annual sales figure reached 5000, and as the VW's reputation for reliability spread by word of mouth, so sales began to accelerate. By 1964, VW Motors could boast well in excess of 100,000 Beetles on British roads.

The view that criticized Nordhoff's 'one-make' policy so heavily in the 1960s became evident as early as the mid-1950s. Many concerned critics insisted that the same pre-war design would not continue to sell year after year, and urged the Wolfsburg chief to change its shape. The car, however, defied its critics and earned itself a reputation for ruggedness and durability the world over—a reflection on the high standards of workmanship in the factory, maintained by the elaborately detailed inspection system initiated by the British and perfected under Nordhoff's rule. By the summer of 1955, Beetles were pouring off the production line at the rate of 1000 a day, and it was obvious that production would have to be decentralized. Volkswagen could never build enough cars to satisfy the ever-increasing worldwide demand in one town, and certainly not in the year that 'Volkswagen of America' was launched, presaging expansion beyond Nordhoff's wildest dreams.

The establishment of VWoA on Fifth Avenue, New York, on 19 April 1955—to promote the Beetle (and to a lesser extent, the Transporter) and raise its previously insignificant 1000 total sales figure—was a move which was to have a far-reaching effect on VW sales in America. Hoffman's New York franchise had been cancelled in late 1953, resulting in a hotchpotch network of independent VW operators dotted all over the country, devoid of any uniform standard or approach to sales and service. Consequently, Nordhoff sent over two of his top salesmen, Godfried Lange and Will van de Kamp, to sort things out.

On paper, at least, the subsequent effect was the proverbial 'overnight success'. The annual sales for 1955 tripled the previous four years' total, although obviously this sudden leap was not entirely attributable to the representatives' efforts. It was the Beetle itself which was finally capturing the attention of the American public. In many ways, the car was an anachronism. Experts thought it much too primitive for American taste in the 1950s—the glory days of Detroit iron. It was noisy and cramped when cars were supposed to be quiet and comfortable; anaemic and frugal when *all* cars had powerful V8 engines and the price of gas did not matter; what is more, it did not even have a gas gauge! It appeared the same each year when earth-shattering up-dates were *de rigueur*, and it did it all without any national advertising (before 1959, anyway). But Americans, Californians in particular, fell in love with the weird little car from Wolfsburg, and soon the little 'Bugs' were everywhere. The boom period had begun.

In next to no time, the 'sincere' American car buyer had to wait anything up to four months to take delivery of his/her new VW, and

Simon Parkinson's 1956 Deluxe was bought new by his late father in the early part of 1957. After clocking up around 70,000 miles in the right-hand-drive Beetle, the Parkinsons waved goodbye to it in 1962—though au revoir would have been far more appropriate. You see, quite by chance almost 14 years later, one of the family happened to spot 547 BTE at the local Datsun garage. It had been reluctantly accepted as a trade-in and looked more than a little sorry for itself. In fact, it was about to be scrapped. But, needless to say, Simon and his dad rose to

*the challenge and two years later it was
back on the road, fully restored. The proud
owner—who had never really worked on
a car prior to this VW—is now an active
member of Britain's Historic VW Club*

anywhere between one and three years
for the newly-released 'glamour Bug',
the Karmann Ghia Coupé. Used VWs
were selling for almost as much as new
ones, and suddenly everyone wanted
one. How did it happen? Of all the
various theories, probably the simplest
is that Volkswagen fulfilled a need
which Detroit had long forgotten
existed; the need for a car that was
cheap to buy and run, small and
compact, light and manoeuvrable yet
solidly constructed, and, perhaps above
all, utterly dependable and trouble-free.
There *were* other European cars which
met most of these requirements, but
VW got their cars to America in
quantity (they arranged for long-term
leases on ocean-going freighters) and
gradually established their world-
famous parts and service network,
thereby eliminating the major obstacle
to owning an imported car in the
United States. And although the Beetle
was certainly one of the cheapest cars
available, it carried none of the social
stigma of a low-priced car within
America's dollar-orientated society. It
could be seen parked between the
finest Detroit 'land-yachts' at the most
exclusive country club. In short,
Americans caught 'the Bug'.

Until August 1955, all Volkswagens
still sported semaphores—the lighted
arrow indicators that pop out from
behind the doors—but many American
dealers had to install fender-mounted
'turn signals' to comply with state
regulations. Conceeding to their
demands, Wolfsburg finally installed
their bullet-style indicators on the US
Export models. Gearshifting was made
easier as well, thanks to a lever moved
forward and cranked back, and dual
'peashooter' exhaust pipes replaced the
former single pipe. Driver comfort
dictated most of the 1956 model

changes: the heater control was moved
forward on the central tunnel for easier
access from wider seats with three-
position backrests. Also, the fuel tank
was reshaped to create a little more
luggage space, while the tail-lights
were moved a couple of inches higher.

On 8 March 1956, VW acquired
the assets of their South African
distributors, where the demand for
Beetles created an exceptionally long
waiting list. This justified a large
investment programme, followed by an
even bigger one in the mid-1960s
when the Uitenhage factory was
expanded for the process of building
wholly South African-made VWs.
VW (Australasia) was a similar
case in December 1957.
Volkswagenwerk became major
shareholders of the existing
concessionaires, and as the market
expanded, so did the number of
Australian manufactured components,
culminating in a 100 per cent
Australian Beetle; likewise the Brazilian
Beetle of 1957 onwards. The Australian
car found its way to such far-off places
as Fiji, the Solomon Islands and New
Guinea. Seven years later, VW
(Australasia) was all Wolfsburg's and,
like the parent company, it went public.

The day of 5 August 1955 marked
what must have been a proud moment
for Volkswagenwerk, when the
millionth Beetle rolled off the
production line. Finished in gold, it
attracted a vast audience and
international news media, earning *Herr
Generaldirektor* the Grand Cross,
Germany's highest civil honour, in
recognition of services rendered to his
country. He was also made an
honorary freeman of the town of
Wolfsburg, following his honorary
professorship at nearby Brunswick
Technical University.

41

Previous page & left
Classic VW drivers have a natural tendency to hoard spare parts, but in some cases it turns into an obsession. Just north of Los Angeles, in a town called Sunland, lies the biggest collection of old VW parts you can imagine. They are owned by a man whose passion for dismantling Volkswagens borders on the eccentric, though he's not in it for a fast buck. Quite the opposite, in fact. Most of his stock— this is just a tiny fraction of it—is not even for sale. Not yet, anyway. He's hoarding it away until the day comes when he can make up his own prices. One man's junk is another man's treasure. . .

Right
Three of a kind: Standard Oval sandwiched between two Deluxe Sunroofs

VW introduced its 1957 model Beetle with tubeless tyres, plus stronger starter and wiper motors. Longevity was to become part of the Beetle legend, with early examples still giving faithful service many years after being built, and whilst being mainly concerned with producing new vehicles, VW never forgot its older models. In 1957 VW purchased its Kassel factory, producing its first 'reconditioned' engine and transaxle units there by mid-1958, as a way of holding down service costs. For 38 per cent of the price of a 'new' engine, VW offered a reconditioned one and soon one in ten German Beetles was powered by an exchange engine.

Just seven years after Nordhoff had been rebuffed by the indifference of potential American dealers, VW's exports to 'Uncle Sam' were bringing in the kind of dollars needed to help turn Wolfsburg into a fully-automated mass-production car plant. At the end of 1957, the company celebrated the birth of its *two*-millionth Beetle—though considerable debate was raging over who actually *owned* the company. Governments at all levels argued the control of VW with various financiers, but it would take another three years to solve the puzzle.

To drive a Beetle from the mid-1950s today, and to compare it with its contemporaries, leaves no doubt as to why the car was such a huge success. The feeling of immense solidity, knowing that nothing is going to break; the light, progressive, quite direct steering; the slightly rubbery but unbeatable gearshift; a ride that absorbs bumps and potholes as if they were not there; the tireless engine thrumming away behind you. There is also, of course, that clap-hands rear suspension that likes to deceive you on slippery surfaces, the sometimes 'vague' front end, and the rather dubious heating system and headlights. But above all, there is that feeling of true quality—not in the 'leather-and-wood' sense, but in the way everything works properly and reliably; and, of course, that unique VW character.

Sometime prior to August 1957, VW, as they said in one of their great ads, called in 'a famous Italian designer' and asked him what changes he would recommend in the Beetle. After studying the car in great detail, he simply said: 'Make the rear window larger.' This Volkswagen duly did, starting with the 1958 model. The Oval-window had disappeared—though certainly not forever.

Above left & far left
One would expect the proprietor of California's best-known obsolete VW parts store to cruise around in something rather special, and sure enough he does: a superb Polar Silver 1957 Deluxe Sunroof. Rich Kimball is one of the world's leading authorities on vintage VWs and his 'BFY' (formerly 'Bugs For You') emporium in Orange County is without doubt the source for all those hard-to-find parts. This pristine Bug is just one of the many classics he has acquired over the years, but it's one of the few he intends to keep. Could you bear to part with a car as nice as this?

Left
Apart from the European-style bumpers, Kimball's beautifully-detailed Oval looks 100 per cent American. Neat!

Above
Amongst the many accessories originally installed by the dealer was a Motometer gauge cluster which replaced the standard speaker grille. The whitewall tyres, mudflaps, gravel guards and tailpipe connector were added after Bob Cheney completed the painstaking restoration

Below
Hood-mounted 'Volkswagen' script was a popular add-on amongst the 900 or so US dealerships in the early 1960s; a 'period' touch very much in vogue today. The enamel Wolfsburg crest became less colourful in August 1959

A li'l ol' Bug from Pasadena .... By the
time this one rolled off the line in 1957,
the Beetle had become America's most
popular imported car. A further $4\frac{1}{2}$ million
units consolidated its position for two
decades

Refurbished early-1957 interior shows centrally-mounted radio speaker grille and 'flat' steering wheel common to Oval-windows. The speaker was moved to the left of the speedo on the '58 models and the steering wheel was 'dished' two years later

Almost two decades between the passing cars, though little difference as far as the layman is concerned. But while the basic technical concept and looks may have remained the same, only one of the 5115 parts which comprise a Beetle remained unchanged: the clamping strip for the rubber hood seal

Wolfsburg rules (1958-1967)

Volkswagen produced its one-millionth Beetle in 1955, its five-millionth in 1961, and its ten-millionth in 1965. And still the world asked for more (another ten million in fact, up to 1981). The Beetle became the most popular car in the world, thanks largely to Heinz Nordhoff's unwavering insistence on 'change only to improve'. While many thought Wolfsburg continued this policy for far too long, today's classic VW enthusiasts have Nordhoff to thank for a seemingly never-ending supply of pre-1968 cars and parts.

Whereas the 1956 model changes had been biased towards driver comfort, several 1957 improvements (for 1958 models) were more technical—stronger main-bearing saddles, enlarged wheel brake cylinders, wider front brake drums, and so on—but of course the major change was the new rectangular-shaped rear window, which almost doubled rearward vision. The windscreen was enlarged simultaneously, by eight per cent. That year also saw the disappearance of the now-sought-after 'W' engine lid, likewise the roller-type throttle pedal which became a treadle. Larger windscreen wipers increased the swept area by 35 per cent, while the front heater outlets were moved rearwards for better heat distribution. All minor changes, but each helping to raise the overall quality of the car.

In 1948, 109 assembly-line workers were needed to produce a VW, but by 1958 that number was reduced to just

Above
Primered Bug, circa 1963, on a side street in Huntington Beach, Southern California

Right
Collector's car: one of the very first 1958 model Käfers to come off the assembly-lines with a rectangular-shaped rear window. The windscreen was also enlarged that year, by 17 per cent

18. That year, Heinz Nordhoff ordered a huge investment programme and automation gradually took over from what were once heavily-manned production lines. Nevertheless, the demand for labour to man the ever-expanding industrial behemoth was such that the factory, once again, began 'importing' Italian workers, who were eventually housed in a specially-constructed Italian village on the outskirts of the town. By 1959, the company could boast one green-coated inspector for every 13 workers, which proved to be ideal 'fodder' for VW's perceptive ad copywriters.

Prior to the appointment of Doyle Dane Berbach as VWoA's ad agency in 1959, Nordhoff sent one of his most respected right-hand men on a mission to America. Carl Hahn, a young economist in the export department at the time and now head of the company, was given the task of putting VW on a par with the Detroit giants. Volkswagen was already Germany's biggest dollar-earner by far, but sales in the US still only accounted for a small

The legendary Wolfsburg crest. Before and during the war, the newly-built 'city of the KdF-Wagen' was known as KdF-Stadt, but on 25 May 1945 the newly-appointed town council (under British control) renamed it Wolfsburg. It was named after the Schulenburg's 16th-century castle, sited nearby

Right
So this '60 isn't 'classic' in the traditional sense, but what the heck! You can bet the driver loves his/her 'Cal-looker' as much as any purist, and it could easily be put back to original specification. See Air-cooled Volkswagens *(Osprey Colour Series) for the full spectrum of modified VWs in sunny California*

percentage of total new car sales in the world's largest marketplace. This full-scale invasion would involve the expansion of the existing dealer network and the general modernization of the entire US operation. Plus, of course, some rather special national advertising. Hahn set up new headquarters at Englewood Cliffs, New

Jersey, and after meeting a reported 4000 fast-talking ad-men, he appointed the Doyle Dane Berbach agency of New York to promote VW sales in America.

The ads they produced through the 1960s literally changed the face of car advertising, creating a look and tone of voice previously unheard of. Whereas every other car ad utilized flattering photographs with suave, debonair drivers and the mandatory admiring female, the humble Beetle was portrayed 'as is'. The copy was self-deprecating as opposed to self-congratulatory and spoke to the reader as though he were an intelligent friend, rather than a distant moron. The Volkswagen did not promise a dream life or a 'rocket-ship ride'; instead, it suggested that the car buyer 'think small'. The car was sincere; it was *real*. Within a year or so, the ads became a conversation piece all over the US and, furthermore, Beetle sales had increased by almost 50 per cent. The campaign was not cheap—it cost $1 million in 1959 alone—but it was effective.

By 1960, Ford, GM and Chrysler were responding to the threat posed by their German rival by introducing a new generation of 'compact' cars. These included the six-cylinder, air-cooled, rear-engined Chevrolet Corvair, a car with all-round independent suspension and a noted absence of brightwork which left no doubt as to which model it was meant to compete with. Within 24 months, imported car sales in the US plummeted. From a high of some 615,000 in 1960, they fell to 340,000 in 1962. But VW sales were left completely unscathed—in fact they rose, to almost 200,000 in

No body or fender repairs needed on this cherry '62 Sunroof, that's for sure

1962. As the compacts inevitably grew in size with each passing year, the unchanging VW was left to pick up an even greater share of the American small-car market lost to its competitors during the initial counter-attack. The Beetle went on to outsell all the domestic small cars, with total sales exceeding five million by the time of its demise in the showrooms. Curiously, when VW built or assembled cars in a number of countries throughout the world, production in the US was never considered. Nordhoff was adamant he should protect the car's 'old-world' quality.

The 1959 model Beetles were almost identical to the 1958s but for an improved fan belt and redesigned clutch springs, but in August 1959 more relevant changes occurred on the Deluxe. VW applied the so-called 'Porsche cure' to the inherent oversteer problem, in spite of Nordhoff's comment a year previously that an anti-roll bar as used on the Karmann Ghia was 'too sporting' for the Beetle. Handling was also further improved by tilting the engine and gearbox forward slightly, thus lowering the swing-axle pivot, while the ride quality was bettered by incorporating more progressive torsion bars. One magazine of the day devoted two paragraphs to the new push-button door handles, while others bemoaned the arrival of the new 'dished' steering wheel with its

'The bucket seats in the front adjust back and forth easily and independently, even while the car is moving. And the backs of the VW's seats recline at three different angles for a change of pace on long trips or a chance for a passenger to snooze . . . .' (Quote from the 1962 VW sales brochure entitled: 'Why is a Volkswagen like no other car on the road?')

Sherm Glas, a former Hollywood film-producer-turned-janitor, believes life is a series of plateaus, and one of the high points in his extraordinary 70 years was when he and his late wife, Lynn, bought the metallic-green Bug pictured here. It was 1966, they had just married, and Sherm had just sold his Sunset Boulevard production company following years of insuperable pressure at the top. He had started out as an errand boy at the Disney Studios in 1937 and had quickly risen through the ranks. As an animator, he was responsible for the creation of the near-sighted cartoon character Mr Magoo, and had a big hand in dozens of other classics, like Tom & Jerry, The Road Runner and Bugs Bunny. Later, he directed and produced movies, TV shows and commercials, and hobnobbed with the likes of Orson Welles and the great Walt Disney himself. But then, in 1966, Sherm gave up the high life to pursue a simple one with his new wife in San Bernardino, far away from the Hollywood glitter. He got a job as a janitor at the Lucky Discount Supermarket and, in his own words, 'found true happiness'. But tragically his happiness turned to deep sorrow in 1984, when Lynn died of cancer. During the last few years, Sherm has been piecing his life back together ('In order to survive I had to revert back to the person she fell in love with'), and in an effort to overcome his grief he has restored their Love Bug to showroom condition and continues to show it at all kinds of VW events. With its 'dealer promotional paintjob' from 'Downtown LA Volkswagen', this Deluxe '66 really is the owner's pride and joy

half-circle horn ring. Several new colours came into being—a sales ploy virtually ignored by Wolfsburg up until this time—and a single padded sun-visor replaced the former green transparent plastic type (front-seat passengers had to wait another year for theirs).

In 1960, most of Europe's other small-car makers could supply a new car in a matter of weeks, but VW dealers were still having to quote a four-month delivery wait for the Beetle. Demand continued to outweigh supply, in spite of the fact that Wolfsburg was turning out almost 4000 cars a day and employing close to 50,000 workers. The Beetle black market which had evolved in America during the late 1950s continued by whatever means possible, and almost two-thirds of German production was officially being exported to other nations. By the early 1960s, VW had notched up sales in no less than 136 different countries, stretching right across Western Europe, on into Asia, Africa, North and South America, and Australia—in fact, all over the world.

Since the British had relinquished control of Wolfsburg in 1949, Volkswagenwerk had remained in the hands of a trusteeship under the auspices of Germany's central government and the State of Lower Saxony. But on 22 August 1960, VW finally became a public corporation. The two official bodies each received a 20 per cent interest in the company's assets, whilst the remaining shares were sold to the public. VW employees were given first option to purchase, limited to nine shares per person plus one as a gift from the company. But despite this gesture, VW suffered its first-ever 24-hour strike at the Hanover Transporter plant, sparking national debate as to whether the burgeoning organization was becoming less 'family' orientated or whether it could be the result of communist infiltration.

There can be little doubt that Professor Nordhoff viewed 1961 as the gateway to a new Volkswagen era. This was the first year in which the company produced a full one-million cars, and total sales since the war surpassed the five-million mark. It was also the year they introduced an all-new body shape—the Type 3 1500 saloon—and made several notable improvements to the Beetle. Changes touched all parts of the 1961 car, but as one of DDB's ads pointed out, 'your eye wouldn't detect them unless we pointed them out'.

The most significant on the Deluxe model was an all-new 1192 cc or '1200' engine with redesigned combustion chambers, higher compression and a subsequent power rating of 40 hp (SAE). The four extra horses were welcome, but the accompanying temperature-regulated automatic choke was not—most who

An 'E' suffix on a British licence plate denotes the car was registered in early 1967, a significant year in the life of the Beetle. Up until that time, the technology that had put man on the moon had had little impact on the people's car, but later that year numerous improvements were announced. These included a 12-volt electrical system, dual-circuit brakes, two-speed wipers, collapsible steering column, and so on, while the more noticeable features were 'upright' headlights and larger tail-lights, new square-section bumpers and an abbreviated hood and engine lid. This all-original E-reg Beetle is one of the last of the old-type classics, a rare right-hand-drive 1200 Standard, owned by Mike and Glynis Croggon from London. They bought the car from its original owner for £1500 when it had covered just 15,000 miles from new, and it came complete with the original sales invoice (£632 total) and a full service history. But 'Stan' isn't the only immaculate Beetle in the Croggons' garage. The lucky couple also own a '62 Deluxe ('Del') and a '68 1500 with an unbelievable 11,000 miles on the clock!

A 1967 Beetle door handle (passenger's)— the last of the push-button type and one of several unique features that year

traded in for the new model complained it wasted fuel. The gearbox was also updated, offering synchromesh on all four forward gears for the first time. All gear ratios, as well as the final drive, were raised slightly, resulting in a top speed of 71 mph and, with quick movements of the new slimline gear lever, one second off the 0–60 mph acceleration time. VW also took the opportunity to redesign the fuel tank on both the Deluxe and Standard models, which resulted in a whopping 65 per cent more luggage space. Likewise, the tail-lights were enlarged for the first time since 1954, and European models eventually lost their semaphores. Meanwhile, at the plant, 1960 was symbolized by the tearing down of the last wartime barracks building, eradicating all evidence of the 'bad' years.

After years of marketing strategy which considered that a redesigned hub cap constituted a major model change, automotive journalists the world over must have welcomed the arrival of the new VW 1500 'Notchback', showcased at the Frankfurt Auto Show in September 1961. In the first issue of Britain's *VW Motoring*, published in November that year, Robert Wyse wrote: 'I took one quick look at the pale blue VW 1500, and then slithered into the driver's seat feeling rather less excited than a brain-washed spaceman about to rocket off on yet another routine, away-from-it-all test zoom. It wasn't until the door clicked shut— solidly, crisply, decisively—that I really believed this was a Volkswagen. Once I had digested the startling truth that a VW is always a VW, no matter what it looks like, I thrilled to every little controlling movement. I was tickled to be the first pressman to drive the 1500 in Britain.' Indeed, in spite of its more contemporary (some would say

'unassuming') body, more powerful 1500 'pancake' engine and twin boots, the car was essentially little more than a Beetle in disguise. But it did go part-way to silencing the critics who believed the Beetle's days were numbered and that Nordhoff was basing an entire nation's export viability on a single design.

Those VW confirmees who traded up to a Type 3 (so-called because the Beetle was the Type 1 and the Transporter the Type 2) benefited from 30 per cent more horsepower, improved riding and handling characteristics (new ball-joint front suspension utilized solid torsion bars as opposed to leaves, plus Type 2 worm-and-roller steering), comparatively excellent driver vision, and a modern spacious interior; plus an accommodating boot at the front *and* the back. The latter was facilitated through the use of a 'flat' 53 hp VW engine with a cooling fan moved to the crankshaft nose, an idea which Porsche's consultancy had first tried three decades earlier, and then suggested again when this type of engine was prescribed for the car in 1959. The overall feel was 'VW', but one you could see out of and drive a little faster—yet still have to open a window in order to shut the door. Until August 1963 only one VW 1500 saloon was available, but that is when the Deluxe version was introduced, the 66 hp 1500S, which complemented the more basic 1500N. From 1966 to 1973, the Notch was available in either 'Standard' or 'Deluxe' trim. However, it is really only the earlier models which are considered 'classic' today. The Type 3 range—the Variant estate, or 'Squareback', joined the saloon on 9 January 1962, followed by the 1600TL 'Fastback' in August 1965—was thought by many to be a possible

eventual replacement for the then-16-year-old Beetle, but the original Volkswagen outlived all its other air-cooled relatives introduced during the 1960s (notably the Type 3 Karmann Ghia and, from 1969 onwards, the Type 4 411, Type 181 or 'Thing', and the VW/Porsche 914). Nordhoff could well retort that those seeking change at any price were mere hysterical stylists!

The 1962 Deluxe Beetle, appearing in parallel with the Notchback, featured such refinements as a fuel gauge, pneumatic windscreen washers and a worm-and-roller steering box, along with the 'Standard' additions which included an easy-to-open spring-loaded bonnet, seat-belt mounting points and larger three-piece tail-lights. A year later, the main selling feature was a modern leatherette headliner in place of the cloth item (plastic seats and door panels had been introduced five years before). German sales actually dropped by eight per cent in 1962, and a Beetle owner survey made later that year found that the overall quality of the car was less than buyers had expected. Clutches were found to be a prime weak point, with 14 per cent requiring replacement all too soon, and the first-ever German car to feature a heater as standard was now considered the least acceptable for winter driving.

Above
A 1500S Notchback, in a Los Angeles suburb

Above right
Brian Johnston's rhd '63 Notchback was 'full of snails, cobwebs and oat leaves' when he discovered it in a Cornish barn, but now it is truly as good as new. The restoration took place over an 18-month period and involved an exhaustive search for NOS (new old stock) parts all over England. There is not a better example on the road today

Nevertheless, one in every three Germans still chose to buy VW.

Domestic sales dropped further in 1963, the year in which Volkswagen celebrated its 25th anniversary, but the figure was more than compensated for by increasing gains abroad. In Britain, gone were the dark days of the early 1950s which had lingered on throughout the decade. The nation was at the start of a new, exciting era which was to mark a fresh chapter for the Beetle in Britain. By 1964—the model year in which the licence-plate light housing was redesigned and the plastic sunroof was replaced by a steel sliding item—100,000 right-hand-drive VWs had crossed the English Channel since the war.

Meanwhile, Beetles began rolling off a new production line in Mexico (*Volkswagen de Mexico*, established on 15 January 1964), while no less than 68 chartered ships were needed to handle exports from Germany. The company had long-since opened another factory at nearby Brunswick for the manufacture of front suspension components and tools, and in December 1964 they opened another, much bigger, plant at Emden, selected for its port facilities. Emden produced most of the Beetles that went for export, while adding about 14 per cent to Wolfsburg's overall production capacity. Around this time, VW also acquired the Auto Union company and promptly turned their Ingolstadt factory into yet another Beetle facility. Sales of the people's car had risen unabated ever since Nordhoff took control of Wolfsburg in 1948, and by 1965 Volkswagenwerk had the largest monetary turnover of any industry in Germany. The annual production figure that year reached a colossal 1½ million, and the *ten*-millionth Beetle made its début in September. Alas, it was the continuing reliance on this model that almost brought the company to the point of bankruptcy in the early 1970s.

Up until 1965, VW had also relied very much on the engineers at Porsche for the design of new models, but steps were taken that year to provide the company with its own research and development centre. This included Europe's most advanced wind tunnel and a new proving ground designed to simulate every conceivable driving condition and hazard—primarily for use in the development of the second-generation water-cooled cars several years later. Other rumours came true in 1965 (August 1964, that is). The Beetle's windows were enlarged all round, thus making door and screen pillars narrower, while a folding rear seat back allowed two passengers to carry a substantial load. Also, the old austere Standard model was deleted and replaced by the 1200A featuring most of the contemporary features. Apart from the usual 'progressive refinements', the VW mystique was largely unchanged. However, more noteworthy up-dates were only 12 months away . . . .

The introduction of the flat-hub-capped 1300 Beetle in the autumn of 1965 marked the first significant power increase in 12 years. This new model, with its 50 bhp power rating, arose because the majority of the Beetle's rivals were, by this time, much faster. German tuners had been the first to build a 1300 cc engine by fitting a 69 mm stroke Type 3 crank to a Type 1 engine, and this was the path that VW itself chose. Along with its new crank, this 7.3 : 1 compression engine had new heads with larger valves and ports, five more fins on each cylinder, and angled manifolds, resulting in a net gain of 20 per cent more power from an eight per cent increase in capacity. The front suspension was also much improved in the 1966 model year, with ball joints replacing link-pins along with better torsion bars and shocks, though the new Bugs were just as sensitive to side winds as their

Above

In contrast to the UK, where a 'cherished' number plate is looked upon as a symbol of affluence, licensing laws in most US states allow freedom of expression for all car owners in return for a minimal fee. Of course, these individual statements are limited by a maximum number of letters and/or digits, and for many it's a contest to see who can come up with the most complex, arcane or esoteric message. But not the owner of this 65 NOTCH. Driving a rare VW in car-crazy California is a statement in itself

Left

Stu Hamill's '64 TYP3VWS on the San Diego freeway, just south of Los Angeles. The owner found this unrestored Notch' while 'treasure hunting' in Germany, and shipped it home full of valuable Volkswagen parts. 'They're good drivers,' says Stu, who spends much of his spare time helping his brother restore early Type 2s

predecessors had been. Also, a heater outlet finally appeared beneath the windscreen and the headlight dip switch was moved to the steering column.

The 12-millionth Beetle appeared in 1966, but it was a triumph soon overshadowed by the recession which began to threaten West Germany. As the government put the brakes on the economy, VW sales on the home front declined to the point whereby the company had to put its massive labour force on short-time working. The introduction of a cheap no-frills 1200 for *Pfennig*-pinchers in early 1967 did nothing to reverse the situation either. By late 1967, Professor Nordhoff, faced with a dwindling profit situation plus increased criticism from both private shareholders and the newly-formed coalition government, became something of a public scapegoat and his health suffered as a result. By mid-1968, however, VW sales began to pick up as Germany came out of its short period of recession—but sadly it was too late for Heinz Nordhoff. Volkswagenwerk's first and longest-

serving *Herr Generaldirektor*, the man largely responsible for the post-war Beetle phenomenon, died in April 1968 aged 69. His successor was Kurt Lotz, a former 'boy wonder of German industry', who eventually resigned in 1971.

In August 1966, when Wolfsburg enlarged the Beetle's engine for the second time in 12 months, the displacement shock was even greater: 1493 cc. VW's engineers combined the 1300 crankshaft with 83 mm bore cylinders to produce 53 bhp at 4200 rpm for the new 1500 VW. Furthermore, they designed a new, squared-off engine lid to mark the occasion (the end of the classic era?). This 1500 superseded the 1300 model in the USA, but Europe continued to offer the 1200 and 1300 Beetles—plus, of course, the 1500 cc Cabriolet, the 1500 cc Type 1 Karmann Ghia Coupé and Cabriolet, and the 1600 cc engined Type 3. The 1967 stateside sedans also incorporated a few of the revolutionary features that were introduced a year later on the European models. The 1500 had front disc brakes (drums in the US), a wider rear track measuring 53.1 in., while all Beetles featured four-bolt wheel fixing, a new pre-heat system (enabling easier starting in cold weather), slimmer side trim, and new rotary door locks preventing the doors bursting open on crash impact.

The changes that followed in August 1967 are too numerous to mention, and from that point onwards the VW engineers consolidated all Teutonic technology in the Beetle—at least, as much as they thought was necessary to keep the car competitive. But all these subsequent refinements could not hide the fact that, with each passing year, the people's car was falling further and further behind its European and

Japanese competitors. Nevertheless, Volkswagen refused to let go of the car that had founded an empire, right up until 19 January 1978, when the last Beetle came off the line at Emden—by which time the water-cooled VWs were leading the way in the world's car markets.

Designed by the inventive Dr Porsche well over half a century ago, then developed by the world's most notorious megalomaniac as a means of political propaganda, the KdF-Wagen, after failing to reach production, disappeared beneath the devastation of World War 2. Had it not been for the dire needs of the occupying forces it would have probably stayed there forever, but the British decided to resurrect the car along with the giant factory in which it would be built. Through one man's vision, that of Heinz Nordhoff, the Beetle became the most popular car in the world, serving the needs of people as diverse in nationality, class and creed as the number of roles it fulfilled during its 33 years of production in Germany. It is a vehicle which became exactly what its original creator intended it to be: a *people's* car. Long may it survive!

All good things come to an end ...

Fun Bugs!

Road & Track once described the Beetle convertible as 'a fun, funny car'. And they weren't joking. With the unique characteristics of the standard 'sedan' *and* a fold-back roof, the Karmann-built Cabriolet will always have a funky kind of charm—what is more, it will always be reflected in the price.

The world's biggest-selling convertible first appeared on the West German market in 1949, though its origins can be traced right back to 1932. That was the year in which Dr Porsche unveiled his first soft-top car sponsored by Zündapp, the motorcycle manufacturer. It was one of three prototypes aimed at the grass-roots market, and although the car bore little resemblance to the Beetle and never actually reached production, it certainly symbolized Porsche's desire to create an open-top vehicle for the mass market. This was further illustrated by his vaguely Beetle-like V2 convertible prototype in 1935.

The first official brochures for the KdF-Wagen included pictures of a convertible, but unlike the saloon and sunroof versions it did not have a fixed price and orders were not even accepted for it. However, the German public got to see the car at the cornerstone ceremony in 1938—likewise Hitler, who sat proudly in the back. It looked remarkably similar to the cars pictured here, though naturally it was painted black. This original prototype (or copies thereof) was well publicized over the proceeding months, but as the political situation worsened the entire emphasis switched to military development and the 'people's' Cabriolet, like the *Wagen*, was shelved.

In the immediate post-war months, the British Army managed to produce a list of what was, in theory, manufactured at the KdF plant prior to the devastation. Beneath the rubble they discovered two convertible Beetles. One was almost identical to the car which transported the Führer in 1938, but the other was the so-called Type 55, the same body design mounted on a Kübelwagen chassis (a dual-purpose 'promo' vehicle perhaps?). A few interesting one-off soft-tops were built in 1946 for the British hierarchy, and one of them, a two-seater roadster belonging to big-wig Colonel Radclyffe, was virtually a pattern for the 'alternative' VW Cabriolet which was later produced by Hebmüller.

Classic Cabs-a-plenty at VW Classic, *held at Irvine, California*

Certainly one of the most desirable drive-fillers any VW buff could wish for: Burton Burton's sanitary 1955 Karmann Kabriolett. *From its mirror-finish black paint to its fully-detailed floorpan, this car can only be described as 'better than new' in every respect (even though pedantic purists might call it 'over-restored'). It is the result of a five-year obsession on the part of SoCal's Tony Moore*

Shortly after Heinz Nordhoff took control of the factory in 1948, he commissioned two old-established German coachbuilders to design and build luxury convertible versions of the Volkswagen, with a view to future mass production. While Josef Hebmüller took care of the now-rare two-seater, Wilhelm Karmann of Osnabrück converted the tin-turtle into a full four-seater Cabriolet that would, over the course of 30 years, capture the hearts of some 330,000 new car buyers.

One of the main problems in the development of the car was the lack of rigidity. The integral strength of the

body was lost as soon as the curved roof was removed (a problem which, presumably, Porsche's design team had not had time to solve). Karmann counteracted this flexing as much as possible by adding longitudinal strengthening sections along each side of the floorpan and reinforcing the door sills. The other problem—the sealing along the top edge of the windscreen—was completely remedied by incorporating a flat-topped screen, as seen on the pre-war prototype. After a great deal of testing, Volkswagen deemed the conversion worthy of a glossy, full-colour sales

brochure, bearing the title *Das VW Cabriolet*, and the car went on sale in July 1949.

With all its fixtures and fittings, the *Karmann Kabriolett*—those were the words on the early quarter-panel badge—was roughly 200 lb heavier than the standard Beetle, and the weight distribution did nothing to improve the inherent tendency towards oversteer. But, surprisingly, its aerodynamic properties were the same—with the top up, that is. With both the top and the side windows down, the drag coefficient went from 0.49 down to 0.60, though the 'cool'

factor more than compensated for this! The luxury Beetle was very expensive at first (DM7500, almost half as much again as a Standard Split), but it sold reasonably well (notably in Switzerland) and the decision was soon made to keep the car as a permanent fixture in the Volkswagen range.

Since it was based on the Deluxe or 'Export' model, whenever the latter was up-dated by the factory, the Convertible (as it was known in the US) also benefited from the latest specifications. However, whereas the age of a classic saloon can be determined to within about five years

'The Volkswagen Convertible with Karmann body is a masterpiece of exterior finish and interior appointments—in fact, it has become the embodiment of common sense in economy and functional design, of engineering leadership and discreet yet fashionable elegance.' (VW Convertible sales brochure, 1956)

by looking at the size of the rear
window, the Beetle buff must have a
sound knowledge of all the subtle
changes in order to tell the exact age
of an old Cabriolet. For example, on 10
March 1953, the last Split-window
rolled off the production line. The
obvious changes to the Cabrio' on that
date? None!

*The Class winners' line-up after the
'Grand Parade' at VW Action, England's
premier event held annually at the Royal
Showground in Warwickshire*

Burton Burton, a wealthy California businessman, owns what is probably the largest private collection of classic VWs in the world—and if not the largest, certainly the finest. The VWs pictured here form just part of his fleet. At the last count they numbered around 30, although by now it's anyone's guess. One thing's for sure, though—there won't be a 'thrasher' amongst them. Burton only collects the very best that California has to offer, and that usually means his acquisition will have appeared on the cover of one of the VW magazines. He has several convertibles, half a dozen or more Buses, sedans of all years, and even an 11-second chopped drag Bug named Frog Guts. But which car does this man—who owns a multi-million-dollar ceiling-fan company and lives with the movie stars in Malibu—enjoy driving the most? A perfectly stock-looking Lotus White '67 Bug ... with a hot 2180 cc engine!

Previous page

This two-tone grey 1957 Cabriolet represents the standard by which all other VW restorations are judged—on the West Coast of America, that is. The car was rebuilt over a 3½-year period by Pheonix's Larry Dustman (before it became part of Burton Burton's collection) at an estimated cost of $20,000. Needless to say, the exquisite convert' is the result of a body-off restoration and everything, but everything, has been replaced, rebuilt or otherwise refurbished. The bodywork alone cost $6000; no Bondo has been used, only lead. The original 36-horse engine looks factory-fresh and the '57 transmission (no first-gear synchro) was also rebuilt and detailed to exacting period specs. Even the animal-hair padding used in the top had to be specially imported from Germany to ensure complete authenticity. It's faultless!

Above

Leather interior (optional in 1957) and Aresma canvas top were Larry's own contributions to the restoration. He also installed several hard-to-find creature comforts like the reclining passenger seat, centre armrest, shifter extension, horn ring, Blaupunkt short-wave radio and the Blumenvasen *in the centre of the dash*

Far left

The under-hood scene is as clean as the rest of the car, and that includes all the areas you'd never normally see. Note the emergency gas can mounted in the spare wheel—yet another sought-after accessory

Above

'Unlike most convertibles that have some sort of compartment where the top stows away when it's down, the Beetle's ragtop just piles behind the back seat, looking for all the world like an old English perambulator—you almost expect to see a nanny pushing the car along.' So wrote Peter Bohr in a feature entitled: 'The 10 best-used car buys between $5000 and $10,000' in Road & Track, *October 1984*

Right

When introduced in 1949, the Cabriolet cost over 50 per cent more than an ordinary Beetle, thus making it a rather 'exclusive' car from the outset. This '58, complete with poodle, has been restored with typical Teutonic thoroughness

Right
*Twin horizontal air intakes replaced the
vertical louvers on convertible engine lids in
1958. The rear window area was increased
by 45 per cent in the same year*

MAR CALIFORNIA CA 85
N0609100
A60VDUB
The Golden State

Left
Cruisin' topless on a warm November morning—what could be more fun?

Below
The venerable Bug is still a firm favourite
with the student population of sunny

California, and those who can afford one
with a convertible top will always be
popular after school ...

Special bodies

The simple but rugged VW chassis challenged countless coachbuilders through the classic years, just as it does today. While many fell under the heading of 'backyard designers', others, like Karmann, Hebmüller and Rometsch, produced beautiful hand-crafted bodies that left a noticeable impression on the sporty car market. But needless to say, these now-highly-prized, VW-based specials were *not* made in fibreglass.

Volkswagenwerk was rarely impressed or even flattered by the proliferating specials that were tacked on to its sacred floorpan back in the 1950s, and only a handful were officially recognized. By far the most successful were those built by Karmann, the largest enterprise of its kind. The craftsmen at Osnabrück had been turning out high-quality car bodies for almost half a century prior to the VW Cabriolet, but it was the firm's association with an equally well-respected Italian styling house, Ghia of Turin, which brought about the best-known coachbuilt VW of all time: the Karmann Ghia.

The introduction of the elegant two-seater Coupé, in October 1955, was perfectly timed. One million Beetles had proved the dependability of the VW chassis beyond question, Karmann's superb craftsmanship was already widely recognized, and there was an obvious gap in the marketplace for an 'individual' but affordable sportscar—somewhere in-between the

Who wouldn't BEHAPPY to own a Karmann Ghia in the land of sun, sand and palm trees, where 'rust' is a rarely-used word?

exclusive Porsche 356 and the standard Volkswagen. The VW Karmann Ghia was an instant success. In fact, its Italianesque lines were so appealing that the initial demand far outstripped supply—especially in America, where waiting lists of two-to-three years were not unheard of.

The painstaking construction process that lay behind each and every Karmann Ghia Coupé and Cabriolet (1957 through 1974) limited the total production figure to just under 365,000. With all its subtle curves, there was no way the car could be built quickly. The bulbous nose, for example, consisted of three separate panels, though there wasn't a seam to be seen anywhere on the body. The 'KG' was a genuine hand-built Volkswagen for the discerning car buyer—or, as VW of America once put it: 'For people who can't stand the sight of a Volkswagen!'

It was the success of Karmann's special-bodied Beetle that prompted Wolfsburg to market a similar alternative based on the Type 3 'pancake-engine' chassis, although it was only similar in name, not in appearance. Known as the 'Razor-edge' Karmann Ghia 1500 (or the Type 343 in Volkswagen's often-confusing model parlance), its styling was radically different to the original Coupé (Type 143) and it was not particularly well received. Nor was it ever exported to the US. The car's nickname emanated from the prominent 'eyebrow' ridge above the four headlights which chief stylist Sergio Sartorelli chose to continue around the waistline. A mere 45,000 Type 3 Ghia Coupés were produced between March 1962 and July 1969. As an interesting aside, Karmann might also have produced a series of convertible Type 3 Notchbacks had they managed to solve

the inherent rigidity problem. More's the pity . . . .

Long before Karmann's special offerings, however, was the 'alternative' VW Cabriolet built by Hebmüller; a truly *classic*-looking two-plus-two roadster. This car (Type 14A) was basically a late-1940s Beetle, but with a bonnet-like deck lid that gave it a beautifully balanced look. But sadly, Josef Hebmüller's factory suffered a disastrous fire soon after the car was introduced and less than 700 were produced. That fire also put paid to a stylish coupé version of the Cabriolet, which was at the finished prototype stage. Nevertheless, there was another open Hebmüller, usually dated 1949 although many had 1948 VW chassis numbers. This was a four-door soft-top Beetle, designed primarily for police duty. A few of the eventual 281 had half-doors in metal but most made do with canvas curtains across the cut-outs. Numbered 18A, this series began at *Karosserie-Hebmüller*, though the last ones were built by Papler due to the fire.

Another interesting four-door Beetle was the purpose-built taxi by Friedrich Rometsch. This was a mildly 'stretched' version of the Deluxe model; an economy limousine complete with rear-hinged doors for fare-paying passengers. Most served their time in Berlin back in the 1950s. Rometsch was also responsible for a *très exclusif* Sports Cabriolet known as the Model Beeskow, now one of the rarest VW 'variants' in the world. It is said that around 2000 hours' skilled labour went into each of these elongated aluminium-bodied specials, and certainly only the well-heeled *Volk* could consider its rather 'special' price. The Beeskow model—so-called after the car's designer, who later became chief engineer at Karmann—was

Above & far right

Bob Gilmore is the lucky fellow who can call this MY 49 VW, or 'a Hebmüller' should he prefer. Only 696 of these 2 + 2 convertibles were produced and only 60 are still known to exist. The Hebmüller, like the four-seater Cabriolet by Karmann, was a VW factory-approved conversion built by an old-established Ruhr coachbuilder of the same name—though for a very short period. In June 1949, less than a year after the prototype was shown, Karosserie-Hebmüller suffered a massive fire which all but destroyed the factory. The destruction was so great, and the insurance settlement so inadequate, that the company never fully recovered from the blow,

completely restyled towards the end of
the 1950s, though Rometsch's
involvement with the people's car came
to a rather abrupt ending in 1961.

Other coachbuilders who gained
some prominence during the early
years were Denzel and Austro Tatra of
Austria, Dannenhauer & Strauss,
Miesan, and Beutler. Wolfgang Denzel
began as early as 1948 with a low,
streamlined 'tub' on a Kübelwagen
chassis. This car won the Austrian
Alpine Rally with hardly any engine
tuning, prompting demand for a small
series. By 1952, Denzel had developed
his own short-wheelbase chassis fitted
with Volkswagen running gear, and in
1954 he won the International Alpine
Rally outright in his 'hot' 1300 VW-
engined special. One of the earliest
VW hot rodders, Denzel later claimed
85 bhp from a 1500 cc engine when a
1.6S Porsche had only 75 bhp. But, like
so many small operations, he could
not maintain the pace and ended
production in 1959 after selling some
300 open, coupé and 'sports' models.
Dannenhauer & Strauss produced a
similar-looking car.

and sadly, in 1950, the model was
discontinued. The example pictured here
was found by its present owner while
serving with the US Forces in Germany,
and was shipped to the West Coast
in 1971

Far left
Hebmüller's long, sloping deck and
disappearing (almost) soft-top really
enhanced the fundamental shape and
character of the Beetle, and would surely
have attracted thousands more buyers had
production continued. Bob paid a paltry
sum for his many years ago, but if he was
forced to sell today it would probably fetch
around $25,000

Austro Tatra, like Denzel, were based in Vienna, but they were fortunate enough to receive the official blessing from Wolfsburg for their open escort vehicle of 1950, the Austro Tatra 114. It was similar to the Hebmüller four-door, and roughly 150 went to the Vienna police, with another 50 or so to their state counterparts. A semi-works number was also given to Miesan, for their ambulance conversion of the Beetle (Model 17). Meanwhile, in neighbouring Switzerland, the Beutler brothers (builders of Porsche's first 356 convertible bodies) produced both practical and sporting models. The former was a Beetle-based delivery van which retained the standard front end, doors, seats and even the rear wings. Their 1954 coupé, on the other hand, dropped all pretence of VW looks. Only the bumpers, hub caps and horn grilles were retained, such that Beutler's bodywork bore more resemblance to an Italian 'exotic' than perhaps any Teutonic creation of the period.

So you see, it was all being done long before the kit car industry came into being . . . .

An early three-spoke steering wheel points this neat ol' Bug towards the beach— where else?

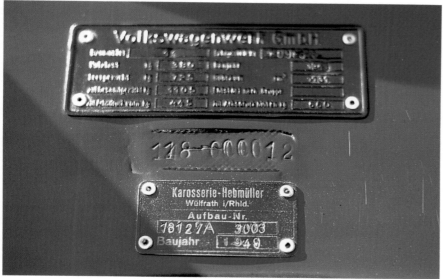

Above

Santa Barbara, SoCal, is home for Steve Herron's immaculate Heb', sporting a two-tone paint scheme which was optional on all early Cabriolets

Left

Hebmüller tag belongs on another example that's alive and well and living in California: Maurey Cole's '49, the 12th one to leave the Wülfrath factory

A Volkswagen made for two. Unlike the
Karmann Cabriolet, the Hebmüller
sacrificed rear seating for a retractable
ragtop—though the token rear seat could
be used when the top was up

*Given the opportunity, what car enthusiast
wouldn't stop and stare at an ultra-rare
two-seater VW Cabriolet?*

An ultra-rare, aluminium-bodied Drews Sport Cabrio', coachbuilt on a Beetle chassis in 1950 and pictured at Autohaus Lottermann

Hebmüller's four-door soft-top was produced almost exclusively for police and fire departments in the late 1940s, and was later emulated by Papler. About 280 were built, the majority with canvas doors, though some were in metal. This example, a '49 conversion owned by Kurt Pflaumbaum, is as 'correct' as you can get. It would have been used mainly for transporting the departmental hierarchy on official processions

Previous page & below
Willi Hofacker's 1952 Rometsch Model Beeskow. This beautiful, three-seater convertible—hand-crafted by Rometsch-Karosserie in Berlin and named after its designer, Johannes Beeskow—was produced between 1950 and 1956. It was a Volkswagen for high society. The very first one was sold to the King of Sweden, and others were driven by the likes of Victor de Kowa, Gregory Peck and Audrey Hepburn, although the aluminium-bodied sportscar was never officially blessed by Wolfsburg. In fact, VW refused to supply the long-established coachbuilders with the rolling chassis and other parts they needed, and they were forced to buy complete cars through their 50 or so employees. The

'banana' (as it was nicknamed by Berliners) featured a soft-top which retracted fully inside the body, a rear seat that was positioned diagonally for more legroom, and front-opening 'suicide' doors. Some 500 examples were sold in total, including a number of hard-top coupés, but only a handful are still known to exist. Name your price, Willi …

Below
A 1953 Dannenhauer & Stauss Cabrio', owned by Andy Luzzi from Switzerland. At the last count, only nine of these Porsche-like coachbuilts were known to exist

Rometsch introduced an all-new VW-based Sport Kabriolett (and coupé) in 1957, around the same time as Karmann unveiled their convertible Ghia. This superb example, a '58 owned by Maribeth and Phil Leadley of Santa Ana, California, shows what a departure it was from the original Beeskow design. With sculptured side panels and tail-fins, a wrap-around windscreen and distinctive chrome trim, the second-generation Rometsch displayed an obvious American styling influence—but it was not as well received as its predecessor had been. Part of the reason was the price. The amount of skilled labour involved in turning out one of these low-volume aluminium bodies was such that the finished product cost a good deal more than even the most expensive Ghia Cabriolet, though it was still cheaper than a Porsche. Various changes were made to this model in 1961, but with the advent of the Berlin Wall later that year, and the subsequent loss of more than half the workforce (now living in the Eastern Sector), Rometsch car production came to a sudden halt. However, the family firm is still in operation today in West Berlin, albeit as an ordinary bodyshop specializing in instant taxi repairs

Above

Globe Automotive Imports Inc. of New York quoted a price of $3300 for the elegant Rometsch (pronounced rahm-etch) in 1958—or twice the price of the Export Beetle on which it was based. However, that included a twin-port/dual-carb Okrasa engine conversion, a fashionable two-tone paint scheme and, moreover, a guarantee of real individuality on the street. Thirty years later, the fake German plate merely adds to the mystique ...

Left

Neat horn button, huh?

Above

Yes, a four-door Volkswagen! Rometsch carried out this Beetle taxi conversion through the 1950s, alongside their special-bodied sportscars. In order to accommodate a second pair of doors, the roof and the floorpan had to be cut in the centre and extended by about 9 in., the original doors were shortened, and new supports were welded in. It was a common sight' all over Berlin prior to the East-West divide. This pristine 1953 example belongs to Herr Lottermann

Top right

The 2 + 2 Karmann Ghia Coupé was first shown to the world's press in the summer of 1955. 'Was it another Porsche?' they asked. No. It was a Volkswagen, built by Karmann, styled by Ghia and based on a mildly-modified Export Beetle chassis. They insisted it was a 'sportscar'. Wrong again. It was a sporty-car, designed for stylish, trouble-free motoring. And so it went on. The enigma of the Karmann Ghia was possibly one of VW's greatest assets during its 19-year production run, certainly as far as their copywriters were concerned. They played on the fact that it was 'a sheep in wolf's clothing' and the 'honest' KG ads they produced during the 1960s were undoubtedly some of their best.

Volkswagen sold 364,398 Type 1 Ghia Coupés and Cabriolets in total, and this photograph shows a few right-hand-drive models that have survived the British climate

Right

When Luigi Segre of the Carrozzeria Ghia was asked to design a car that would be both elegant and distinctive among German manufacturers, the Italian's efforts evolved into a beautiful form which met with worldwide approval. Belgian photographer Serge Briton, the lucky guy behind the 'wheel of this 1956 coupé, is among those who rave about the style more than 30 years on

Overleaf

Karmann corner—another view from Sunland, California. And this is nothing compared to what's stashed behind locked doors!

*Surf boys and Ghia on the Pacific Coast
Highway in the summer of 1986*

Inset
'There's a little bug in every Karmann Ghia' was one of the amusing headlines used by Doyle Dane Berbach, VW's American ad agency, back in the 1960s. The KG was both longer and wider than the Beetle, and a full 6 in. lower. This one's a pre-1958 model, recognizable by its low-set headlights and small 'nostril' air intakes

Previous page

Chip Wimer of Beaumont, California, says he got hooked on VWs back in high school, when a dual-Weber'd 'Cal-Bug' was far more appealing than any show-winning restoration. But that was then, as they say. Nowadays, his preference is for all-original rarities like his very own 1964 Karmann Ghia, in blue and white. This model (Type 34) was never officially exported to the United States, and Chip, who runs an owners register and liaises with like-minded enthusiasts in Europe, estimates there are less than 2500 left in the world today. His must be one of the cleanest

Left
Licence-plate light of a Type 3 Karmann Ghia

Right

Bill Makepeace, co-proprietor of 'Bill & Steve's' (Type 3 specialists) in Bellflower, Orange County, uses this 1964 1500S Ghia for daily transportation. It is one of the few Type 3 Ghias that has spent its entire life in the Golden State. Back in the early 1960s, the demand for VWs in California was so great that a certain SoCal dealer took at least one vacation a year in Germany in order to buy and ship home more Bugs. In 1964 he also brought back this Terra Brown Karmann Ghia, convinced that the car's unusual appearance would appeal to at least one showroom-browser. And sure enough it did. The story goes that a man bought the 'fancy import' as a present for his wife, who, by late 1986, was getting too old to climb in and out of the low-slung driver's seat. Consequently, Bill snapped up the rust-free KG and has enjoyed driving it every day since. The location is McDonalds, at Downey, California—one of the original eight hamburger stands operated by the McDonald brothers, Dick and Mac

Left

With its long deck, skinny roof pillars and pronounced accent lines along each side, the 'Razor-edge' Ghia is not everybody's cup of tea, styling-wise. But thankfully, like the 45,562 original buyers, there are still those who consider it to be a beautifully balanced design, one that is well worth preserving. Mike White's right-hand-drive example was actually white with a black roof when it left Osnabrück in 1965, but somewhere along the line someone decided to personalize it. However, it's all-original, apart from the paintjob, and has never yet been turned away from a concours d'élégance in England. In fact, it's a regular show winner and for that reason the owner never drives it during winter. Can you honestly blame him?

The old Bulle

Like its primeval counterpart, the ox, the flat-faced VW Transporter was built to carry close to its own weight— though this fact had no bearing on its popular German nickname, the *Bulle* or 'Bulldog'. The association with this animal is purely visual and, though somewhat obscure, you don't have to be a Type 2 enthusiast to realize why it came to be. Nor to appreciate the vehicle's intrinsic *Volkswagen* character.

The evolution of the Type 2 range can be traced right back to 1946 and the notepad of Dutch entrepreneur Ben Pon. Early that year, Pon travelled to Wolfsburg to discuss the possibilities of becoming sole VW concessionaire for the Netherlands and noticed a rather odd-looking vehicle shuttling parts around the factory. It was little more than a platform on wheels; a basic utility vehicle built up on a Beetle chassis but with the driver's seat and controls mounted at the rear, directly above the engine. This creation obviously inspired Pon, for a year later he returned to the Wolfsburg Motor Works with definite ideas of what a marketable 'transporter' could look like. What is more, the sketch he made whilst discussing these ideas with Colonel Radclyffe (chief of all light

engineering industry in the British Occupation Zone) was almost a blueprint for the 'box-on-wheels' as we know it. His accompanying notes stated that the vehicle should have a 1500 lb carrying capacity and that the driver and controls should be positioned at the very front of the vehicle.

Development of the one model which had *not* been part of the pre-war Porsche line-up began soon after Heinz Nordhoff took control of the factory in 1948. Like Ben Pon, the new management anticipated the need for such a vehicle long before the people called for it. The first prototype was based on an ordinary Beetle chassis, but it was quickly discovered that a more substantial sub-structure would be required. This took the form of two main frame rails running lengthways, with five cross-members between the axles. The standard Beetle wheelbase was retained, however, though the

bodywork was welded rather than bolted to the chassis, thus making the Transporter VW's first vehicle with unitary construction.

The Transporter's running gear was basically the same as that of the people's car, except for heavier-duty front suspension and Kübelwagen-type reduction gears at the outer ends of the driveshafts. These provided the necessary ground clearance, as well as a little extra 'push' from the 1131 cc 30 hp engine. Inside, by positioning the spare wheel and fuel tank within the engine compartment, some 162 cu. ft of centred loadspace was created, which amounted to roughly two-thirds of the entire volume of the 'box'. Furthermore, a 4 ft square double side door made the vehicle simple to load at the kerbside with up to 1650 lb of cargo, as well as allowing easy access for passengers. The characteristic V-shaped split windscreen was found to be the most favourable design,

Left
Abandoned Bus, at Bad Camberg

Right
'Bullet' front indicators replaced semaphores on American-specification Type 2s in 1956, the same year that production of the entire Transporter range was transferred from Wolfsburg to a purpose-built plant in Hanover. European Buses switched from semaphores to flat-lens indicators in 1962

following a succession of wind-tunnel tests. Throughout the experimental stages, the Transporter was known as the Type 29, but the second digit was dropped just before Nordhoff introduced the all-new Volkswagen to the world on 12 November 1949.

The very first production model Type 2 (February 1950) was a Kombi, a dual-purpose people/cargo carrier featuring windows along each side and a pair of easily-removable bench seats behind the cab section. Along with the Commercial or 'Panel van', these were the only models offered until May 1950, when the Microbus was introduced. The Micro was much like the Kombi, but with a two-tone paintjob and better upholstery, it was more expensive. By the end of that first year, Transporters were rolling off the Wolfsburg assembly-line at the rate of 60 per day.

Above right

It may look like new, but Willi Lottermann's Dove Blue Transporter is believed to be the second-oldest Type 2 in existence; one of 9541 made during the first year of production. Apparently, the 30-horse motor of this '50 seized after just three years' service and the vehicle was subsequently laid to rest until Herr Lottermann heard about it in 1985. And where's the oldest Bus in the world? It's sitting round the back of Willi's VW dealership, awaiting full restoration

Right

A Beetle instrument cluster (fitted with an 80 km/h speedo) was the extent of forward furnishing within the very early Type 2s

Tonny Larsen's 1953 Microbus must be one of the highest-mileage vehicles in Denmark—as well as one of the longest-surviving Volkswagens. This Bus spent the first 17 years of its life registered as a taxi, then went through numerous changes of ownership before Tonny acquired it shortly before Christmas in 1985. Of course, in a climate where corrosion has long-since eaten up most 1950s cars, much welding was necessary before the old 'barndoor' (pre-'55 model) could be repainted and shown off at various events organized by the VW Veteranklub Danmark. But don't think it's a show-only vehicle—the owner drives this Type 22A every day during the summer months

Left
The VW Bus did not receive a rear bumper until late 1953, so this engine is probably a 36-horser—52 mph with the pedal on the metal!

Previous page

Different *is one word for it,* bizarre *could be another—whatever, there's no mistaking Burton Burton's amazing Krankenwagen. This restored but somewhat customized 1958 ambulance is one of the biggest crowd-pullers on the West Coast show circuit, and it's easy to see why. San Bernardino's Dennis Rose had the notion to revamp this ex-Canadian 'sick car' (that's how it translates!) and he did so with the utmost attention to detail. The accoutrements include a siren, a revolving blue light, spotlights and, inside, an ex-gynaecologist's chair and a stretcher complete with 'drips'!*

Left

Volkswagen added the ambulance to their Transporter range as long ago as 1951, and with it came a certain feature that became standard on the other models four years later. A rear door or 'hatch' was obviously an important requirement—for the loading of patients on stretchers—and it necessitated moving the spare wheel and fuel tank from the engine compartment so the latter could be reduced in height, likewise the huge 'barndoor' (early engine cover). This enabled a hatch to be placed above it, though on the ambulance it hinged downwards, just like an oven door

Right

The Deluxe Microbus, Sondermodell or 'Samba' was VW's top-of-the-range Transporter. It came with a huge, sliding canvas sunroof, small 'sky' windows along each side, and extra trim. This '61 is owned by Huntington Beach (Surf City) resident Steve Pontius, and he likes to think of it as 'practically stock'. That is, more practical than stock, thanks to a hopped-up, late-model 1600 cc motor. The custom paintjob and Safari windows also do nothing to spoil the original character

June 1951 saw the introduction of the now-sought-after eight/nine-seater Deluxe Microbus or 'Samba'. This model featured such luxuries as a huge canvas sunroof, windows *all* the way round, and four skylights along each side of the roof—not to mention some pretty fancy (by Volkswagen standards) exterior trim. The dash, which had previously been a single pod type, was made full-width on the Deluxe (to accommodate a clock and an optional radio), while a carpeted rear luggage tray behind the rear seat was surrounded by rather ornate, chrome-plated railings. It was the top-of-the-line 'people carrier' and remained so until the major face-lift of 1968.

An ambulance version of the Microbus appeared at the end of 1951, and with it came a certain feature that would later become standard on the other models—namely, a rear hatch. This change called for a relocation of the fuel tank and spare wheel, and new homes were found above the transmission and behind the front bench seat. Also that year, the first-ever VW Camper conversion (by Westfalia) was made available, and those who dared to be different could order one with a chromed front bumper (rear bumpers were not standard issue until late 1953). Almost 12,000 Type 2s left the factory in 1951, but the following year the production figure was almost doubled.

The single-cab pick-up was added to the range in the summer of 1952. The cab section was basically the same as a regular Kombi, but from the seat back the layout was obviously revised. The 'people's truck' featured a completely level bed, $8\frac{1}{2}$ ft long and 5 ft wide, complete with 15 full-length hardwood runners to protect the cargo. The hinged side gates could be lowered by the driver in a matter of seconds,

Left

Glass in each rear corner distinguishes the 23-window Deluxe from its younger, 21-window brother

Right

August 1963 saw the disappearance of the 'post-box' rear window, a characteristic feature of all vintage Buses (apart from the Samba). The larger window was installed in a hatch that was 30 per cent wider

thereby creating a flat-bed facility for extra-wide loads. Another strong selling point was the 'weatherproof locker' situated beneath the bed. This gave the truck a further 20 sq. ft of secure load area, sufficient space for most tradesmen's tools; and for those tradesmen wishing to protect the entire contents of the pick-up, there was even an optional canvas-top assembly.

On the same day as the Beetle's rear window changed to a one-piece oval shape (10 March 1953), Volkswagen finally decided to give the Deluxe Microbus a rear bumper. This decision obviously met with much approval, since every Transporter had one by the end of that year—except the pick-up, which had to wait until April 1954. The advent of the mighty 36-horse 1192 cc engine soon after was also a blessing for Type 2 drivers. That meant they could run flat out at 52 mph— 4 mph faster than before! Volkswagen even raised the maximum speedo reading from 50 to 60 mph, in case of strong tail winds . . . .

By 1955, the tireless Transporters were firmly established as good, economical work vehicles, and as sales of all Volkswagen models were escalating rapidly, plans were drawn up to build a new purpose-built plant for the manufacture and assembly of the entire Type 2 range. The site chosen

for this monument to Germany's post-war industrial growth was just outside Hanover, very close to Wolfsburg, and it opened in March 1956, covering a million square metres.

Two notable changes occurred on the range 12 months before the transfer. One was at the front, the other at the back. An overhead ventilation system was built into the cab roof which resulted in a distinct 'eyebrow' above the windscreen. This was due to the redesign of the forward roof to include a fresh-air intake duct. Meanwhile, at the rear, the giant 'barndoor' engine cover compartment

was reduced to a fraction of its height following the decision to incorporate a rear hatch similar to that installed in the ambulance almost four years before. It was an improvement which also provided a further 8 cu. ft of loadspace. Other up-dates in 1955 included a full-width dashboard on all models, smaller-diameter wheels (16 to 15 in.), a two-spoke steering wheel in place of the original three-spoker, shorter engine cooling vents (thanks to a redesigned fan), and a walk-through option which utilized two single seats up front instead of the standard bench. All *functional* improvements.

VW were faced with a stack of back orders for all their Transporters by the time the new factory was completed, though 1957's annual production figure of some 92,000 units all but satisfied the demand. The following year there was yet another addition to the family: the ever-so-practical double-cab (or 'crew-cab') pick-up. It was essentially a half-Kombi, half-pick-up, with seating for six adults and a rear cargo area measuring almost 6 × 5 ft—plus a large storage area beneath the rear seat. However, like all the models at this time (apart from the Micros), it was only available in one of three colours—red, blue or light grey—or

otherwise bare primer, to be painted in company colours at the point of delivery.

As the demand came from every area of commerce, VW offered several variants utilizing doors of every description, a variety of interior heights, and special pick-up beds for every conceivable application. For example, there was a truck which featured a tip-up bed like that of a dumper truck used on construction sites, and a high-roofed Panel van for furniture suppliers and the like, featuring $2\frac{1}{2}$ ft of extra 'ceiling' space. The VW's reputation for versatility, longevity and all-round good design

spread worldwide, and on 2 October 1962 the one-millionth Transporter rolled off the line. True to their 'good' public image, Volkswagen donated it to the UNICEF Foundation.

Long-established manufacturers of light commercial vehicles were, by the early 1960s, feeling the full effects of VW's presence in the market. In fact, not only had Volkswagen taken a sizeable slice of the 'commercial' cake, they had also created a new market for dual-purpose transportation. The passenger-carrying Buses accounted for almost 45 per cent of total Transporter production in the first decade; consequently, imitations began to

All stacked up and ready to go!

appear on both sides of the Atlantic.
But as always, VW's clever copywriters
used this fact to the company's
advantage, reacting with headlines like:
'Look who's following us.' In effect, the
imitators merely served to increase the
sales of the real thing. Moreover, they
confirmed the wisdom of Nordhoff's
original prediction: 'When a box-on-
wheels is the basic need, a box-on-
wheels is the perfect answer.'

Following the 36 to 40 hp power
increase on the 1961 models, 1962
brought a fully-synchronized gearbox
and several minor improvements. Inside
the cab, the visors were changed from
a cardboard-like material to padded

plastic and a fuel gauge finally became
standard on all models. Larger, flat-lens
front indicators replaced the 'bullet'
type; likewise, the tail-lights were
completely redesigned. Generally
speaking, VW applied its latest
technology to the Type 2s before the
Beetle, and this was proved in August
1962 when Transporter buyers were
offered the 1500 cc engine; a sliding
door was also available at that time on
request. A year later, as the wheel
diameter was reduced, yet again, to
14 in., the rear hatch was made
significantly wider (incorporating a
Deluxe-size rear window), and as a
result the Samba lost its rear quarter

windows. Type 2 specifications stayed
much the same for the next few years,
while VW were busy tooling up for
the all-new, second-generation
Transporters introduced in August
1967.

In just over 17 years, Volkswagen
produced some 1.7 million split-screen
Bulles and distributed them to over 140
countries. Long live *the real Bully!*

Above & above right

Charlie Hamill has what you might call a penchant for early Type 2s, and this, his restored 1960 Panel van, is nothing short of perfection. Since 1983, this SoCal resident has owned no less than 30 Split-screens (seven of which are still in his possession), and has established 'The Bus Stop' (used/NOS Bus parts, Safari window restoration/installation, etc) as a means of subsidizing his hobby. This Dove Blue '60 was found in Phoenix, Arizona, with just over 42,000 original miles on the clock and relatively little body damage, but it took a full six months to restore it to its former glory. Needless to say, it's one Bus he intends to hang on to ... forever

Right

The cleanest Type 2 engine compartment in the world! This original motor is an 'intermediate' 1192 cc, offered on the Transporter line from late 1959 to mid-1960, shortly before the output was raised from 36 to 40 bhp (SAE). It featured many unique parts that are now all but impossible to find

Above

As well as the original double cargo doors and walk-through options, Charlie's van now features a two-speed overhead fan and 'cool' opening Safari windows. Most of the Safaris that 'The Bus Stop' supplies come from Central America where, it is said, eight out of ten Buses have them installed

Above right

'Who puts raincoats on pick-ups? Volkswagen.' That was the headline for a VW ad which depicted a single-cab pick-up like Charlie Hamill's—but unlike the one in the ad, Charlie's '58 never gets caught in the rain. You see, his is an all-original, 9000-miles-from-new gem; a precious piece of VW history that is rarely exposed to the elements. Charlie paid $6000 for the truck in 1986, complete with a canvas 'raincoat' which the original owner had never even unfolded

Left

*300-miles-a-year average since new!
Charlie's pick-up spent the best part of 30
years locked away in an underground
garage and is now only ever driven to
SOTO meets close to his home in Orange
County, Southern California*

This is the vehicle that sparked off Burton Burton's obsession for collecting old Volkswagens: a 1962 Samba, owned by his good friend Melissa Van Siclen. When they first met several years ago, Melissa (known as 'Mudflaps'!) had been driving this old Bus for 12 years and was extremely attached to it—in spite of the fact it had been stolen and stripped at one time and was in pretty poor shape. However, its condition soon changed once Burton became interested. Following the proverbial 'double-pump rejuvenation', the couple drove the Bus to the first annual VW Classic event, and by the end of the day the enthused Pasadena businessman had acquired his first-ever Volkswagen, a beautiful '56 Bug. The rest, as they say, is history . . .

Above
' "It looks like a bus." "I wouldn't be caught dead in it." Do these sound familiar? Your wife is not alone. It is hard to convince some women what sense the VW Station Wagon makes . . . .' (Early 1960s VW ad for the nine-seater Deluxe Microbus)

Overleaf
No less than 460 pre-1968 Type 2s turned up at the 4th Anniversary SoCal SOTO (Society of Transporter Owners) meet; the happening for Split-screen freaks

'Once you get into air-cooled, that's it, you're hooked,' says Tony Angel, the driver of this 1965 Devon-conversion Camper. Tony bought the Bus back in 1983 as a means of touring Scotland 'on the cheap'. Unfortunately, it blew a piston before the owner and his family encountered any dramatic scenery, but they managed to limp all the way back to Kent (some 300 miles) on three cylinders. Needless to say, FDG 421C has been 'one of the family' ever since